Pseudocode Algorithms and Pascal Programming for CSEC Exa

O'Neil Duncan, PhD.

ISBN-13: 978-1516898084

ISBN-10: 1516898087

Table of Contents

Contents

Problem Solving using Computers...6

Characteristics 11

IPO Diagrams..16

Basic Elements of an Algorithm 16

Variables..16
Data Type 16

Pseudocode 19

Basic statements 19
Arrays and Loops 25
Array Basics 25
Arrays 26
Array declaration and creation 26
Storing Values and Accessing Elements 27
Arrays and Loops 28
The Temperature Program..28

Linear Search 29

Implementation 29

Programming 33

Task 3...33

Topic: 35

•   **simple calculations** 35

1. **The WHILE Statement** 39
2. **For Statement**..43
Format 43

11   Comments: 43
12   Begin 45
End   45
13   Begin 46
End while 46

14   Flow Charts 49
15   Flow charts and sub processes 55
Data Flow Diagrams..61

CASE STUDY: MASQUERADERS...67

Summary 72

Programming Languages 73

Programming Language Generations...75

Translators 77

Steps in Implementing a Program..78

PROGRAMMING IN PASCAL 79

Pascal Editor and Library 82

Pascal Programs...87

Variables and Constants 87
Data Types..88
Character...93
String 94
Implementing Pascal Code 97
Conditional Branching..99
Menus   106
Loops (For, While, Repeat Until Loops)..107
Arrays   115
Subroutines 116
Procedures and Functions 117
Function 117
Parameter Passing...117
Return Values 118
Searching and Sorting...118
SORTING..121
SELECTION SORT 122
BUBBLE SORT 123
Quick Sort...125
FILES   126
1. Data Files..126
Random Access Files 130

TRACE TABLES..136

PASCAL ERROR CODES 138

CASE STUDY: MASQUERADERS 141

CASE STUDY:

We will be using the following case study as part of the SBA project in order to understand how it all works. This case study will be used in Chapters -2, 6, 7 and 8.

Carnival has long been a traditional cultural festival in several Caribbean territories. Every year, thousands of costumed masqueraders parade through the streets, dancing to the pulsating sounds of steel band, calypso and soca. Most of these revelers register to participate in the band of their choice months before festivities begin. Organizers of these bands must utilize management and organizational skills in order stage a successful event. As a bandleader of one these carnival bands, you are required to utilize suit a Word processing, spreadsheet, database management as well as a programming application to design and implement computer-based solutions to the tasks involved in the management of your carnival band.

Unit 2: Problem Solving and Program Design

Chapter Objectives:

In this chapter, we will learn:

- How to approach problem solving using algorithms.
- How to test and validate algorithms
- How IPO diagrams can be used to break down a problem.
- How variables and constants can be used in an algorithm.
- About the basic elements of an algorithms
- About the characteristics of an algorithm.
- How to represent an algorithm in a different way: Pseudocode, Flowchart, and Data Flow Diagrams.

Problem Solving:

Life is not so simple. It is not straightforward. There are always problems which confront us in our daily undertakings. The smartest way to get out of a problem is to find a solution for it.

Problems can manifest in many form. Sometimes, they arise out of bad decisions; most other times, these problems are circumstantial. When problems are circumstantial, it means that there is no fault of ours but still a problem is a problem.

So, when we encounter a problem, how do we approach it? How do we solve it?

Let us consider a simple scenario for example. We are given a mathematical problem to solve. What do we do here?

The first step in any problem solving procedure is to define the problem. In this scenario, we state word to word what the question demands. We define what the problem is.

The next step is to analyze the problem. This means we understand what we have stated. For example, in this scenario, we understand what the question is, we note down the data that is given to us, and then we look at how this data is going to be used in solving a problem. Once this data is assimilated, we need to process it and every process requires a step-by-step execution.

However, we must remember that there are many possible solutions to a given problem. For example, consider the mathematics problem we have been given. The textbook book is just one possible way of solving the problem. If we search anywhere else, we may find other ways to do the same thing. How then do we decide which way is the best way to deal with the problem? The answer is simple. We analyze which solution is difficult for us to understand. Sometimes, a textbook solution would be the one we fail to understand. However, we may find some other way which would seem to us easier than the one we have been taught in the classroom. Once we find the easier way, we choose that solution.

Once we have chosen the way, we solve the problem. Use the data in the way that is required. Once done, we verify whether the result is what is expected by the teacher. If it is then we know that we have committed no mistakes.

The same concept applies to every mundane activity of our life. Problem-solving is an art but it also requires a logical mind.

Problem Solving using Computers

Computers were invented to supplement the human mind. A computer is faster, efficient, and less prone to errors. Not to mention, it is versatile.

Since computers have such excellent qualities, they have become an asset to problem-solving. Almost everything is digitized these days and there are quite a few places where the computer system is not used. Generations of computers have passed and with the technological advancements, it is only getting better. The computers have become speedier and more efficient.

As we all know, a computer system is built upon a hardware system and runs with software. A software is nothing but a collection of coded language which is designed for a specific purpose. Some software are application software while a few others are built to interact with the hardware. However, let us ask ourselves whether these softwares are coded just like that or whether a process is followed?

Just like we solve problems in general, we could also employ the same procedure while solving problems using a computer. We cannot just code the software based on a title. To build anything, we need a foundation and to build a foundation, we need data.

So let us now see through the steps in problem solving

Step 1: Define the problem

The first step is to be clear on what we want. So, define the problem. If there is no clear and concise definition of the problem we are about to solve then there can be no possible solution. Everything will be murky and chaotic. For example:

Problem: An array is given to us with as many as ten elements. We are required to find a specific element within the array and display its position.

Now that we have defined the problem, let us now go to the next step.

Step 2: Analyze the problem

The next step as usual is to analyze the problem. Here we see what data we have been given and how we can use that data to achieve the goal.

Data: The data given to us are the ten elements in the array and the element we require to be searched.

After analysis, we hunt for possible solutions.

Step 3: Find possible solutions and choose the best solution

The next step is to scour out possible solutions, evaluate them and then choose the best solution.

To choose a solution for a problem we are going to solve using computers, we need to look at the complexity of the solution. This is done by using the Big O Notation. The Big O notation analyses the solution by predicting how much memory the solution will use and how much faster the solution will compute.

Solution:

We find that there are two possible ways to search for an element in an array. They are:

1. Linear Search

2. Binary Search

One of the most important and most frequently occurring operations on a collection of entities is the location and retrieval of an entity in the collection. For example, in a student registration system, an academic advisor may have to find a student record for a student with a given name or identification number in order to inspect their academic record. Or a student may wish to access information on a particular course, identified by a course code, to determine whether they have passed the prerequisites and perhaps who is teaching the course. In both cases, one can assume that the program maintains a collection of entities, student records and course information records respectively, and that it has to retrieve a particular entity from this collection.

There is a considerable amount of work on making retrieval of records faster, particularly when the collection is stored in a file on a secondary storage device such as a hard disk. One way of achieving faster retrieval of a record from a file is through the use of so-called indexes. However, a discussion of indexes will have to wait until a later date. For our current purposes, we will only explore searching for an entity in a list which is kept in main memory.

The simplest way of searching for and retrieving an entity from a list is through linear search. As the name implies, linear search involves going through the list element by element until one either finds the element one is looking for or one reaches the end of the list. It should be clear that the average complexity of linear search is n where n is the number of elements in the list. If the element is the first element in the list, then one merely needs to make one comparison. On the other hand, if the element does not occur in the list, then one will have to go through all the elements in the list before one can determine that the element one is looking for does not occur in the list and one therefore has to make n comparisons.

On average, however, the element one is looking for will occur somewhere halfway down the list, i.e., in position n/2, and one will have to make n/2 comparisons to find the element. Since one ignores the constant when determining the complexity of an algorithm, it should be clear that the complexity of the algorithm is n.

While a complexity of O (n) is in general not too bad, it is important to realize that, for large lists, retrieving an element through linear search becomes a time consuming affair. The question therefore is whether one can do better. Fortunately, the answer is yes, provided that:

The list is sorted

One can access each element in the list in a single step

One knows beforehand where the midpoint of the list is.

Assuming that these three conditions are true, one can use an algorithm known as binary search. Binary search involves repeatedly cutting the part of the list that one is looking for in half, until one either finds the element one is looking for, or the part of the list that one is looking has become empty. Binary search starts by comparing the element one is looking for with the element mid way down the list. If the list is empty, one can return failure immediately; if this element is identical to the one we are looking for, then we immediately. Otherwise, and assuming that the list is sorted in ascending order, if the element one is looking for is smaller than the element in the middle, one repeats the process for the first half of the list; if the element is larger, then one repeats the process for the second half of the list. Clearly, if the list is sorted in descending order, then this has to be reversed.

So we have come across two search methods. Depending on complexity analysis, we choose a solution. For many, linear search would be an easier way of searching through the array.

Step 4: Create algorithm

Now that we have chosen our solution, we will now create a way to implement this in the form of an algorithm.

An algorithm is a step by step method of performing calculations and operations. Algorithms find usage in:

- Calculation
- Data Processing
- Automated Reasoning

An algorithm is an effective way and consists of well defined instructions. The process of creating an algorithm involves three stages:

1. Determining the input data.

2. Processing the input.

3. Outputting the processed input.

Input. This is data that needs to be entered by the user in order to solve the problem. Input data is known by the user, hence something which is unknown and is to be determined through processing, cannot be part of the input.

How do I look for the input?

(a) Check for key words or phrases e.g. **read, , enter, accept, prompt the user** etc.
(b) Determine whether **the processing** or **the output** is dependent on **an input**. If so, then the input is necessary.

If an input is required, count the number of different input entities and determine whether an entity has to be entered more than once. Assign a **variable name** to each type of input.

Processing. This involves

- calculations,
- repeating program instructions and
- selecting segments of the program at times.

How do I know if calculations are required?

a) Check for the key phrases such as **calculate percentages, discounts, Totals** and **averages; counting values - determine the number of times, determine the frequency etc.**
b) Check for the need to **add, subtract, divide** and/or **multiply**.

N.B. These calculations may be implied by the output that is required.

Output. This is information that will be generated as a result of

i. solving the problem
ii. Or it may be messages- called prompts that appear on the screen to facilitate processing.

Example:

1. Write a program that *prompts* the user for *three numbers* and *outputs* the *sum of these numbers*.

(Note that the keywords in the question are underlined)

Analysis:

What is the input?	Processing:	What is the output?
three numbers - stored in the variables Num1, Num2 and Num3.	Input values Calculation: the sum i.e. add A, B and C Output results	sum of the numbers inputted - stored in the variable **Sum.**

Code:

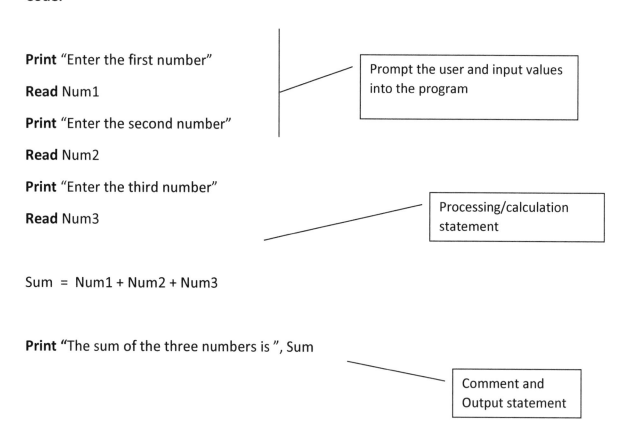

Print "Enter the first number"

Read Num1

Print "Enter the second number"

Read Num2

Print "Enter the third number"

Read Num3

Sum = Num1 + Num2 + Num3

Print "The sum of the three numbers is ", Sum

Prompt the user and input values into the program

Processing/calculation statement

Comment and Output statement

Characteristics of an algorithm:

We should take care of the following characteristics before getting to designing any algorithm:

1. Finiteness: An algorithm must end after a finite number of steps. Each step of an algorithm must only take a measurable amount of time.

2. Definiteness: Each step must be precisely defined. The action must be rigorous and unambiguous for every case of input data.

3. Input: An algorithm can have zero input. It can also have one or more inputs but the number has to be a finite number.

4. Output: An algorithm can have one or more outputs. However, the requirement of one output is compulsory. Zero output means we cannot know the solution provided by the algorithm.

5. Effectiveness: An algorithm should be effective. Each operation performed in an algorithm must be basic and simple.

Let us now come back to our search example scenario. Say, we selected the binary search algorithm.

We can define binary search as a List behavior as follows:

```
Binary Search
  Input:   Element e
  Process:
    result <- false
    start <- 0
    end <- length()
    middle <- (start + end)/2

    WHILE (start < end AND result = false)
      midelement <- retrieve( middle)

     IF (e == midelement)
       result <- true
     ELSE
```

```
            IF (e < midelement)
            THEN
                end <- middle - 1
            ELSE
                start <- middle + 1
            ENDIF
        ENDIF

        middle <- (start + end)/2
    ENDWHILE

    RETURN result
```

Output: true if e occurs in the list, false otherwise.

It is perhaps interesting to point out that there is an obvious way in which this algorithm can be reformulated recursively. We define a recursive version BSRec as follows:

```
BSRec
    Input: Element e, start, end
    Process:
      IF (start == end)
      THEN
          RETURN false
      ELSE
          mid <- (start + end)/2
          midelement <- retrieve( mid)

          IF (e = midelement)
          THEN
              RETURN true
          ELSE
            IF (e < midelement)
            THEN
                RETURN BSRec( e, start, mid - 1)
            ELSE
                RETURN BSRec( e, mid + 1, end)
            ENDIF
          ENDIF
      ENDIF
```

Output: true if e occurs in l, false otherwise.

In order to illustrate that how the algorithm works, assume that we are trying to find whether 7 occurs in the list

0 1 2 3 4 5 6 7 8 9 10 11 12 13 14 15 16 17 18 19 20

We will use the following conventions: The part of the list that we are considering will be colored red, while the value of mid will be colored blue, while start and end will be underlined. Since we initially consider the entire list, we therefore start with:

0 1 2 3 4 5 6 7 8 9 10 11 12 13 14 15 16 17 18 19 20

We notice that the list is 21 elements long. Therefore, mid is 10:

0 1 2 3 4 5 6 7 8 9 10 11 12 13 14 15 16 17 18 19 20

We now compare the element that we are looking for, 7, with the element we find in mid and notice that it is smaller. We therefore set end to mid − 1 to give us the following list:

0 1 2 3 4 5 6 7 8 9 10 11 12 13 14 15 16 17 18 19 20

Since mid of the part of the list that we are looking at is 4, we compare 7 with 4 and notice that it is larger. We therefore give start the new value mid + 1, resulting in the following list:

0 1 2 3 4 5 6 7 8 9 10 11 12 13 14 15 16 17 18 19 20

However, the element we now find at mid is equal to the value that we are looking for. We can therefore return true. It is perhaps instructive to repeat the process for an element that does not occur in the list, say 21. Below we simply give the state of the list on each iteration through the loop using the same conventions as in the above example:

0 1 2 3 4 5 6 7 8 9 10 11 12 13 14 15 16 17 18 19 20
0 1 2 3 4 5 6 7 8 9 10 11 12 13 14 15 16 17 18 19 20
0 1 2 3 4 5 6 7 8 9 10 11 12 13 14 15 16 17 18 19 20
0 1 2 3 4 5 6 7 8 9 10 11 12 13 14 15 16 17 18 19 20

After this iteration, we see that start and end get the same value and we return false. Notice incidentally that we discovered that 21 did not occur in the list after only 5 iterations. We determine the complexity of the algorithm from the iterative version. If we assume that each of the operations in the algorithm, such as retrieving an element from a given position or determining the length of the list can be achieved in a single time step, something we will come back to later, it should be clear that the complexity of the algorithm is exclusively determined by the number iterations through the WHILE loop. All the other statements in the algorithm have a complexity of (1). Unfortunately, determining the number of times we go through the loop is not straightforward. We therefore approach the question a little differently. Notice that if we go through the loop once, we can only find the element in the middle. Finding any other element requires at least one further iteration. However, if we go through the loop twice, we could in principle locate three elements, namely the one in the middle or, depending on the value of the element in the middle of the list and the value of the element that we are looking for, the one in the middle of the first half of the list or the one in the middle of the second half of the list. Following the same argument, in three iterations through the loop, we would be able to locate 7 possible elements. We can represent this graphically as follows, where the number indicates the number of the iteration in which the element could be located:

```
0 1 2 3 4 5 6 7 8 9 10 11 12 13 14 15 16 17 18 19 20
              1
      2                   2
   3     3         3         3
   4  4  4    4      4    4   4      4
```

We can represent this in tabular form as follows:

Number of iterations	Number of elements discovered
1	1
2	3
3	7
5	15

It should not be too difficult to see that we can generalize this to say that in m comparisons, we can find $2^m - 1$ elements. Unfortunately, this equation is in a sense the wrong way around. We have discovered how many elements we can find in a given number of iterations. What we would like to determine is how many iterations it takes to find any of a given number of elements. A little thought will show that what we need is the inverse of the function given above, and the inverse of raising 2 to the power of m is to take the logarithm with base 2. In other words, we can conclude that the binary search algorithm requires log(n) iterations to find any element in a list of n elements. You are also reminded that for even for n of relatively modest size, log(n) is considerably less than n. For example, log(1000) is approximately 10. In other words, finding an element in a list of 1,000 elements will at most take 10 time units when one uses binary search, while it might take up to 1,000 time units if we if we use linear search. Moreover, every time we double the size of the list, binary search would merely require 1 additional time unit, while for linear search the running time would double.

So, while there is no doubt that binary search leads to a far superior performance as far as retrieval from a list is concerned, it is good to remember that binary search is possible only if:

- The list is sorted
- One can access any element in the list a single time unit
- One knows the length of the list beforehand

The reason for the first condition will be obvious. When one compares the element one is looking for with the element in the middle of the list, then one moves to the first half of the list if the element one is looking for is smaller than the one in the middle, and to the second half of the list if the element is larger. Clearly, this is completely predicated on the fact that the list is sorted. If the element is smaller than the element in the middle, then, because the list is sorted, if it is anywhere in the list, it must be stored before the one that one is looking at.

The reason for the second requirement will be clear as well. In the binary search algorithm, one has to be able to retrieve elements from any position in the list. Thus, the first line in the WHILE loop in the iterative version is:

midelement <- retrieve(middle) .

Clearly, the only reason that the algorithm can be of order log(n)) is if this particular line in the code has a complexity of (1). Since this is true for an array implementation of a list, binary search is possible only if we have implemented the list as an array. It is important to realize that this limits the use of binary search to find an element in a list to those applications in which an array implementation of the list is appropriate, i.e. when one can predict beforehand how many elements the list will maximally contain.

The reason for the third requirement will also be clear. In order to initially determine the middle position in the list, we essentially divide the length of the list by 2. This in turn can only be achieved if we can determine the length of the list in a single step. Since this is possible in an array implementation of a list in which one maintains a pointer to the end of the list, it follows that binary search can be used effectively only in an array implementation of the List class where we maintain a separate pointer to indicate the end of the list.

Even though binary search may be applicable only in one of the many different implementations of the List class that we looked at, it is nevertheless an extremely powerful retrieval technique. It is also clear that sorting the list is essential if one is to use binary search.

Step 5: Test and Validate the Algorithm

Once we have created the algorithm, we manually work for logic and consistency. We want to know whether the algorithm we have created is giving the result we require. In our scenario, we want to know whether the element we want searched in an array is really being returned.

Testing the algorithm is done by creating test cases. Test cases include sample data which we assign to the elements of an algorithm and check it by manually tracing through it to see if the resultant output is what we require.

Step 6: Implement the algorithm in a programming language

The next step is we convert this algorithm into a coded language. The language is chosen depending upon the environment the program is going to be used and many other factors. When an algorithm is written in a programming language, the result is called as a program.

Examples of programming languages include C, Pascal, C++, Java, etc.

Step 7: Run the program

The program, once written, is now sent to a compiler.

A compiler is a system software which converts the program written in a programming language into an executable file which can then be run.

Step 8: Document and maintain the program

Documentation of a program is very important. There are two kinds of documentation:

1. External Documentation: Involves user manuals, etc.

2. Internal Documentation: Involves comments, etc.

IPO Diagrams:

IPO is an acronym for Input-Process-Output. These diagrams find usage in the analysis of a problem. It is a functional model and acts like a conceptual schema of a general system. This diagram helps in the identification of the inputs given to an algorithm, the outputs generated by the algorithm and the process required to convert the input into the refined output.

Basic Elements of an Algorithm
Variables:

A variable is a name associated with a particular location in memory used to store data. Variable names should be meaningful. Examples: arg, firstname, sum etc.

Some variables are reserved; hence cannot be used.

Data Type:

A variable has the ability to store different types of data.

There are four important data types that we must know about:

1. Long (integer, number with no decimal point)

2. Double (real number, number with decimal point)

3. String (text)

4. Boolean (true or false)

Declaring Variables:

We declare variables in order to reserve space for the data in the memory unit and to inform the computer system what kind of data will be stored.

Initializing a variable

Variables have to be initialized so it gets the correct starting variable. However, it is not compulsory for all variables.

Example: Sum:=0, Counter:=0.

Constants:

Constants are usually fixed values. Examples: 5, 'abc', etc.

They are normally assigned to variables or used in computational operations.

Literals:

A literal is a notation for representing a constant in the source code of a programming language or an algorithm. They are often used to initialize variables.

For example:

Int a = 1;

A:=1;

Ways to Represent Algorithms:

There are many ways to represent algorithms. However, these four are the most prominent.

1. Narrative

2. Pseudocode

3. Flowchart

4. Data Flow Diagrams

Narrative:

A narrative is a way of representing an algorithm in precise English language.

For example, let us consider doing a linear search for an array:

Narrative Example for linear search:

1. Declare Array A of type Integer with 10 elements.

2. Declare Num and found of type Integer.

3. Declare counter I of type Integer and initialize to 0.

4. While I is less than 10, read array element A [I].

5. Increment I by 1 and goto step 4.

6. Read Num.

7. Initialize I to 0.

8. While I less than 10, perform the following step:

9. if A [I] is equal to Num then Initialize found to 1 otherwise increment I by 1.

10. Goto step 8.

11. if found = 1 print "Element found" otherwise print "Element not found."

12. Stop.

Pseudocode:

Pseudocode can be termed as an informal high level description of an algorithm. It uses the same conventions as a computer program but its purpose is to be easily understood by humans rather than a machine. People usually find pseudocode to be easily readable and understandable than programming language code. It follows all the key principles of algorithm design.

Example:

Write a program that will allow *input the of the name and price* of an item in a supermarket. The program will *calculate* and *output* the *name of the item* and the *new price* after a 15% discount is given.

Solution:

What is the input?	Processing:	What is the output?
• The name of the item -	Calculations:	• The name of the item

stored in the variable **Name**.	• the discount given - stored in the variable **Discount**.	
• The price of the item - stored in the variable **Price**.	• The discounted price of the item – stored in the variable **NewPrice**	• The discounted price of the item

Pseudocode:

Print "Enter the name of the item"

Read Name

Print "Enter the price of the item"

Read Price

> Input statement: Prompt the user and input values

Discount = Price * 0.15

NewPrice = Price – Discount

> Processing/calculation statements

Print "The name of the item is ", **Name**, " and the new price of the item is ", **NewPrice**

Programming
Task 1

Topic: Programming Basics:

Basic statements	Assignment/storage statement	data type
Input and Output statement	Calculations • percentage • discount etc.	data conversion

1. Write a program that asks the user for her name and gives the response: "<the given name> is a beautiful name."

Plan:	**Code:**
declare the variables	var NameGiven: string;
ask for name (input)	readln(NameGiven);
give the response (output)	writeln(NameGiven,' is a beautiful name');
end the program	End.

2. Write a program that asks the user for her age and responds: "You are only <the age given>! I thought you were at least <the age given + 2>."

Plan:	**Code:**
declare the variables	var Age,NewAge: Integer;
ask for age (input)	readln(Age);
calculate new age (processing)	NewAge = Age + 2
give response (output)	Writeln('You are only', +Age+, _
	'I thought you were at least' +NewAge+ '.')
end the program	End.

3. Write a program that asks the user for an amount in CI dollars and outputs the equivalent in US dollars. (NB: To convert CI dollars to US dollars, multiply the CI amount by 1.20.)
   Required format of output: if the amount in CI dollars is 60, then the output would be: "60 CI dollars is equivalent to 72 US dollars."

4. Write an algorithm which prompts the user to enter the price of an item and which calculates and prints the new price after a discount of 12%.

5. Write a program that asks for the radius of a circle and prints out the area and circumference.
   Note that area = pi * r * r, circumference = 2 * pi * r and pi = 3.14159.

   Required format of output if the radius is 5: "The area is 78.53975 and the circumference is 31.4159 when the radius is 5."

6. Write a program that first asks for the first name and then asks for the last name of the user. The program should print out the last name followed by a comma, a space and the first name. So, if the user type "Elvis" and "Presley", the program should output "Presley, Elvis".

7. A certain account at a bank earns compound interest on a yearly basis, and has no deposits or withdrawals. The balance after a year has passed is given by the formula:
   This Year's Balance = Last Year's Balance * $(1 + \text{Interest Rate})^N$, where Interest Rate is given as a decimal fraction. (For example, 25% must be entered as 0.25.)

   Write a structured algorithm to do the following:

(a) Request the user to provide the interest rate as a decimal, the number of years to compute interest for, and the starting balance.

(b) Read in the interest rate R, and the value N which is the number of years to compute interest for.

(c) Read in the starting balance.

(d) Compute and display the balance, including the interest, after N years have passed.

8. Write pseudo code to interchange the values in two variables A and B.

Write a program that asks the user for her first name, age, favourite colour and favourite food. The program should output a full sentence on this form "I agree with you Susan, blue is a beautiful colour. When I was 17 I ate a lot of pizza too."

Topic: *Selection/Decision Statements*

Example of a Selection or decision statement:

- **IF** statement
    - A statement for testing conditions to allow for decision making. The **IF** statement *conditionally* executes a statement based upon the **truth** value of a condition.

The **IF** part is executed if the condition (*information that should be kept in mind when making a decision*) is *true*, the **ELSE** part (*if present*), is executed if the condition is *false*.

In programming, conditions are written as Mathematical expressions.

Examples of conditions:

Description	Written in programming as
Single conditions	
• *A is grater than B*	**A > B**
• *price is less than or equal to 25.00*	**Price <= 25.00**
• *mark is equal to PassMark*	**Mark := PassMark**
• Number is not equal to zero	**Number <> 0**
• Name is not equal to Mary	**Name <> "Mary"**
• Price is at least $10	**Price => 10**

• Price is at most $100	**Price =< 100**
Multiple conditions	
• First name is equal to John and age is less than 37.	**FirstName = "John" And Age < 37**
• First name is equal to Sue and the hobby is sailing .	**FirstName = "Sue" or Hobby = "Sailing"**
• Mark between 50 and 80	**Mark > 50 and Mark < 80**

Format: this form of the IF statement is used when the problem definition gives two distinct options to choose from.

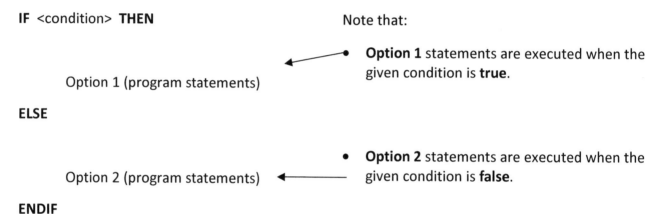

IF <condition> **THEN**   Note that:

       Option 1 (program statements)   • **Option 1** statements are executed when the given condition is **true**.

ELSE

       Option 2 (program statements)   • **Option 2** statements are executed when the given condition is **false**.

ENDIF

Example 1:

Write a program which accepts the price of an item. The program should calculate and print the discounted price of the item. A **15% discount is given for prices above $100.00 and a 10% discount for all other prices**.

Analysis:

INPUT	PROCESSING	OUTPUT
Price of an item (to be stored in the variable **Price**)	1. **Two** choices are presented which implies that an IF statement is required. The **condition** for selection is: Prices above $100.00 i.e. **Price >**	Discounted price of the item (to be stored in a variable called **DiscountPrice**)

| | 100.00;

Price > 100, 15% discount given;

Other prices, 10% discount given;

2. Calculate the discounted price | |

Solution written in pseudocode:

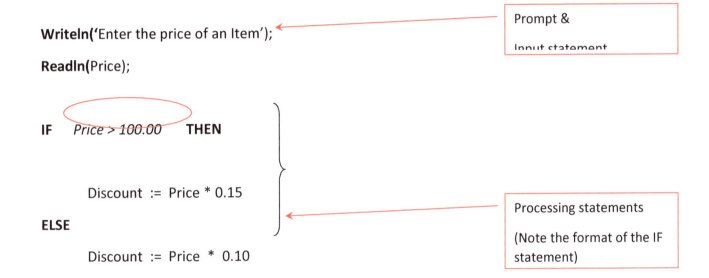

Writeln('Enter the price of an Item'**);**

Readln(Price**);**

IF   *Price > 100.00*   **THEN**

            Discount := Price * 0.15

ELSE

            Discount := Price * 0.10

ENDIF

DiscountPrice := Price - Discount;

Writeln('The price of the item after discount is', DiscountPrice**);**

Prompt &

Input statement

Processing statements

(Note the format of the IF statement)

Output statement

Condition

Example 2

A bonus of $1500.00 is given to employees who were absent for less than 4 days in a year. The bonus is added to the salary to arrive at the total income. Read the days absent and salary and output the employee's income.

Analysis

INPUT	PROCESSING	OUTPUT
Two inputs: 1. Number of days absent (to be stored in the variable called **DaysAbsent**) 2. Salary of the employee (stored in a variable called **Salary**)	1. IF statement: The **condition** for selection is: Days absent less than 4 **DaysAbsent < 4, bonus given;** **Otherwise, no bonus given** 2. Calculate the Total Income	1. The employee's income (stored in a variable called **Income**)

Solution written in pseudocode:

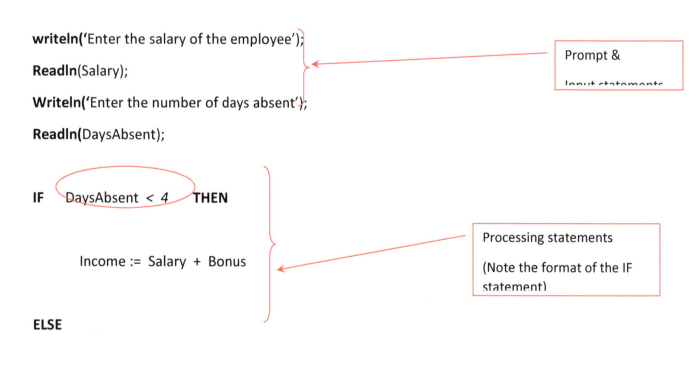

writeln('Enter the salary of the employee'**);**

Readln(Salary**);**

Writeln('Enter the number of days absent'**);**

Readln(DaysAbsent**);**

Prompt & Input statements

IF   DaysAbsent < 4   **THEN**

            Income := Salary + Bonus

Processing statements

(Note the format of the IF statement)

ELSE

            Income := Salary

ENDIF

writeln('The employee's income is', Income**);** ← Output statement

↑ Condition

Note that if more than two options are given, then we can use a combination of **IF** statements called **embedded IF statements (to be discussed)**.

Arrays and Loops

Array Basics

Consider the following interaction (input in **red**):

```
How many days' temperatures? 7

Day 1's high temp: 45

Day 2's high temp: 44

Day 3's high temp: 39

Day 4's high temp: 48

Day 5's high temp: 37

Day 6's high temp: 46

Day 7's high temp: 53

Average temp = 44.6

4 days were above average.
```

We need to be able to read each input value twice: once to compute the average (a cumulative sum) and again to count how many were above average. We could read each value into a variable, but we don't know how many days are needed until the program runs, so we don't know how many variables to declare.

We need a way to declare many variables in one step and then be able to store and access their values.

Challenge: Is it possible to solve the above problem using only the techniques from the previous notes without using arrays? How?

Arrays

An *array* is an object that stores many values of the same type. An array *element* is one value in an array. An array *index* is an integer indicating a position in an array. Like `Strings`, arrays use *zero-based indexing*, that is, array indexes start with 0. The following displays the indexes and values in an array with 10 elements of type `int`.

index	0	1	2	3	4	5	6	7	8	9
value	12	49	-2	26	5	17	-6	84	72	3

Array declaration and creation

The syntax for declaring an array is:

***type*[ ] *variable*;**

This just declares a variable that can hold an array, but does not create the array itself.
For example, to declare a variable, `numbers` that can hold an array of integers, we would use:

```
int[] numbers;
```

Since arrays are objects, we create arrays using **new**.
When creating an array, you specify the number of elements in the array as follows:

***variable* = new *type*[*length*];**

For example, to create an array of 10 integers:

```
numbers = new int[10];
```

We can combine the two operations of declaring and creating an array:

***type*[ ] *variable* = new *type*[*length*];**

Our example would become:

```
int[ ] numbers = new int[10];  // an array of 10 ints
```

This would assign the following array to the variable `numbers`.

index	0	1	2	3	4	5	6	7	8	9

value   0   0   0   0   0   0   0   0   0   0

Each element in an array is initialized to zero, or whatever is considered "equivalent" to zero for the data type (`false` for `boolean`s and `null` for `String`s).

Storing Values and Accessing Elements

The syntax for storing a value in an array element is:

variable[index] = expression;

For example:

```
numbers[0] = 27;
numbers[3] = -6;
```

would change the `numbers` array to:

index   0   1   2   3   4   5   6   7   8   9

value   27   0   0   -6   0   0   0   0   0   0

The syntax for accessing an array element is:

variable[index]

where the index can be any expression that results in an `int`. For example:

```
System.out.println(numbers[0]);
if (numbers[3] > 0) {
    System.out.println(numbers[3] + " is positive");
} else {
    System.out.println(numbers[3] + " is not positive");
}
```

When you declare an array, each element of the array is set to a default initial value. For integers, the default value is 0. What do you think the default value is for doubles?

Activity: Array default initial values

Write a program that declares a `double` array of length 4, prints the values, assigns a value to each element, and prints the values again.

Now do the same thing for an array of `String` elements.

Arrays and Loops

We can use an integer variable as the index of an array. If we use a for loop to count from 0 to the highest index, then we can process each element of an array. For example, the following code would sum the elements in the `numbers` array.

```
int sum = 0;
for (int i = 0; i < 10; i++) {
    sum += numbers[i];
}
```

We start at 0 because indexes start at 0. We end just before 10 because 10 is the length of our `numbers` array, and the last index is one less than the length of the array.
[Arrays provide many opportunities for *off-by-one* errors because of the way indexes work.]

If we changed the `numbers` array to have a different number of elements, this code would no longer work. Fortunately, Java provides a easy way to obtain the length of an array, by appending `.length` after the array variable, for example:

```
int sum = 0;
for (int i = 0; i < numbers.length; i++) {
    sum += numbers[i];
}
```

Notice that for arrays we do not use parentheses after the length.
This is different from the way the length is done for strings.

Activity: Initialize and Show Integer Array
Write a program that inputs the length of a `int` array from the user and assigns 1 at index 0, assigns 2 at index 1, assigns 3 at index 2, and so on. One loop should assign values to each element of the array. A second loop should print the values of the array with spaces between the values.

Activity: Initialize and Show Double Array
Write a program that inputs the length of a `double` array from the user and a value for initializing the array. One loop should assign the value to each element of the array. A second loop should print the values of the array with spaces between the values.

The Temperature Program

Consider the interaction at the beginning of these notes. Here is pseudocode that follows the sequence of interactions, using an array to manage the values that the user enters. Note that we can't count how many elements are above the average until we have computed the average, and we can't compute the average until we have input all the elements.

1. Input the number of days from the user.
2. Declare and create an `int` array with the number of days as its length.
3. For each index in the array:
A. Input the temperature from the user.

    B. Store the temperature in the array at that index.
4. Initialize a sum to zero.
5. For each index in the array:
    A. Add the value at that index to the sum.
6. Calculate and print the average.
7. Initialize a counter to zero.
8. For each index in the array:
    A. If the value at that index is greater than the average:
    A. Increment the counter.
9. Print the counter.

We could have combined the first two loops into one loop, but it is cleaner to do them separately. Here is the program that corresponds to the pseudocode.

Linear Search

A linear search is the most basic of search algorithm you can have. A linear search sequentially moves through your collection (or data structure) looking for a matching value.

Implementation

```
function findIndex(values, target) {

  for(var i = 0; i < values.length; ++i){

    if (values[i] == target) { return i; }

  }

  return -1;

}

findIndex([7, 3, 6, 1, 0], 6)
```

Programming
Worksheet

Topic: Programming - Selection/decision statements

So far we have looked at three program statements. One of them is an input statement. Identify the other two.

1. _____

2. _____

Program statements can be categorized into one of the following groups: input; process; output;

For each of the following statements, identify its category:

Statement	Category
Writeln(Newprice);	
A = 2 * P + Q	
Readln(Score);	
Discount := Price * 0.5	

Write the condition for the following statements:

■ A day is considered hot when the temperature is above 32ºC and normal otherwise. Output the appropriate message.

_____

____

■ Output the message tall for boys with heights of at least 5' 9".

_____

____

Write the selection statement for the following scenario:

■ If A is bigger than B, output the difference between A and B. In all other cases, output the sum of A and B

Write the analysis and algorithms (in pseudocode) to solve the following problems: -

1.   A credit union pays 4% interest on shares that are greater than $25,000.00 and 3% on all
        other shares. No interest is paid on deposits.

        a)   Read a share and a deposit.
        b)   Calculate the interest amount
        c)   Calculate the total savings (**total savings := shares + deposit + interest amount**).
        d)   Output the interest amount and total savings.
Analysis:

Inputs:	Processing:	Outputs:

Pseudocode for the algorithm

2. Input the mark that a student obtained for each of three subjects. If the average mark is less than 60, output "fail" otherwise output "pass".

Analysis:

Inputs:	Processing:	Outputs:

Pseudocode:

3. Read the quantity sold and unit price for an item and the money received. Calculate the total cost. If the money received is greater than or equal to the total cost, output the amount of money due to the customer. Otherwise, output the comment "Account receivable".

Inputs:	Processing:	Outputs:

Pseudocode:

Topic:

- **Conditions:** if-then – else statement,
- Indenting
- Logical expressions

Summaries you should know before you do this lesson: logical terms, logical expressions, if-then-else-endif, if-then-elseif-elseif-else-endif, indenting if-statements.

1. Write a program that asks the user for her name and gives the response "David is a beautiful name" if the name is "David" and otherwise gives the response "X is an ugly name", where X is the name given.

Plan:	Code:
Declare variables	var NameGiven: string;
	readln(NameGiven);
Input name	If NameGiven = "David" then
	Writeln(NameGiven, 'is a beautiful
Compare input with "David"	name')
If same as David, print "<input" is a	Else
beautiful name	Writeln(NameGiven, ' is an ugly
Otherwise, print "<input> is an ugly	name')
name"	Endif
	End.
End program	

2. Write a pseudocode algorithm to read two numbers and print the lower value. (Assume the numbers are not equal)

3. Write a structured algorithm to read in two numbers and print the higher value. (Assume the numbers are not equal)

4. Write an algorithm to read in TWO numbers into A and B. The algorithm should store the smaller in A and the larger in B, and then print A and B. (5 marks)

5. Write an algorithm to read an integer value for SCORE and print the appropriate grade based on the following:

SCORE	GRADE
80 or more	A
less than 80 but 65 or more	B
less than 65 but 50 or more	C
less than 50	

Write a program that asks the user for the capital of Venezuela. If the right answer is given, it should respond: "Yes, you are right! Caracas is the capital of Venezuela." If the answer is wrong, it should say: "No X is not the capital of Venezuela." where X is the answer given.

Topic:
- simple calculations
- selections

1.   A hired car is charged at $25.00 per mile for the first 100 miles and $10.00 for the rest, plus a fixed charge of $17.75. Write a structured algorithm which prompts the user to input the distance traveled. The program should calculate and print the total charge.

2.   Write an algorithm to read the amount of sales made by a salesman. He is paid $500.00 plus a commission of 10% of sales. Calculate his commission and output his sales, commission and total pay.

3.   Write an algorithm which prompts the user to input the length and width of a room. Calculate and print the total cost of carpeting the room. One square metre of carpet costs $45.00.

4.   Write a structured algorithm which prompts the user to input two numbers which are stored in A and B. If B is 0, output the message "You cannot divide by zero", otherwise divide A by B and output the result.

5.   An examination consists of two papers. A student fails if his or her percentage for either paper is less than 50. It should output the information with the words "Pass" or "Fail" as appropriate.

6.   Write a structured which prompts the user to enter the price of an item and the discount percentage given on the item. The program should print the discounted price of the item.

7.   Write a structured algorithm which prompts the user to input to unequal numbers which are stored in A and B. It should subtract the smaller number from the bigger number and print the result.

8. Write a structured algorithm which prompts the user to input to unequal numbers which are stored in A and B. The algorithm should store the larger number in A and print both A and B with suitable comments.

9. Write a structured algorithm which prompts the user to input to unequal numbers which are stored in A and B. The algorithm should print the smaller number.

Answer the following questions in the space provided.

1. Explain the following terms:

(a) Compiler

-

_____

_____

_____

_____

_____

_____

(b) Source Code

_____

_____

_____

_____

_____

_____

(c) Object Code

_____

_____

_____

_____

_____

_____

2. What is produced as a result of the compilation process?

_____

_____

_____

_____

_____

_____

3. Name two programming languages that have to be compiled before the code can be executed.

_____

_____

_____

_____

_____

_____

4. State one benefit of the compilation process.

_____

_____

_____

_____

_____

_____

Loop Structures

There are times when writing programs, that we want the computer to execute a set of statement several times. To do this, we need a loop structure to instruct the computer

- what to repeat and
- how often to repeat these steps

There are basically two types of loop structures/statements

Note: *Use this statement when the problem that you are solving gives a condition for stopping/terminating the repetitions.*

1. **The WHILE Statement**

- Executes a series of statements as long as a given condition is **True**.

Format of the while statement:	Explanation of terms:
	condition
While *<condition> do begin*	an expression that evaluates to **True** or **False**.
	Program statements

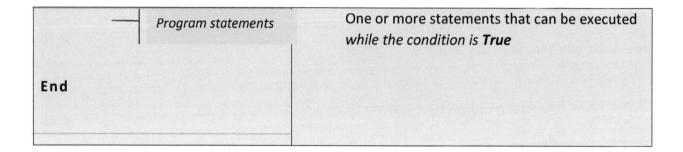

| Program statements | One or more statements that can be executed *while the condition is* **True** |

End

How does the while statement work?

When a while statement is encountered by the computer, it checks the truth value of the condition. If *condition* is **True**, all program statements (as shown above) are executed until the **End** (endwhile**)** statement is encountered. Control then returns to the **While** statement and *condition* is again checked. If *condition* is still **True**, the process is repeated. If it is not **True**, execution resumes with the statement following the **end** statement.

Example 1:

Write a program to input a set of prices. The list will stop <u>when the user enters -1</u>.

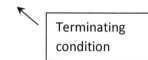

Terminating condition

Solution:

```
Writeln('Enter the price of the item');

Readln(Price);


WHILE Price <> -1 do begin

        Writeln('Enter the price of the item');

        Readln(Price);

END;
```

The following examples illustrate use of the **While** statement:

Example 2: Write a program that accepts the price of a set of items <u>terminated by an entry of 9999</u>. The program output the total price paid by the customer. It should also output the highest price entered.

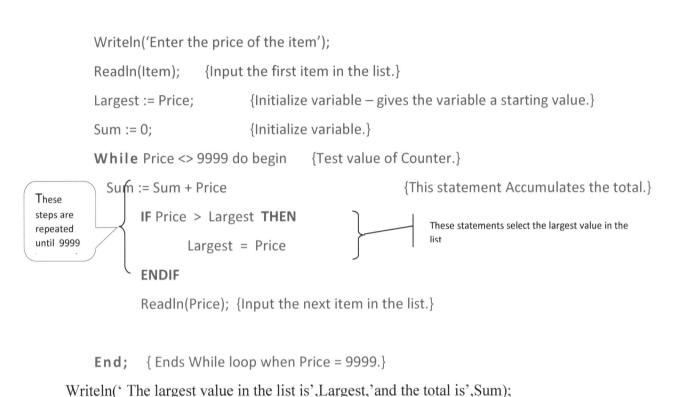

```
Writeln('Enter the price of the item');

ReadIn(Item);      {Input the first item in the list.}

Largest := Price;           {Initialize variable – gives the variable a starting value.}

Sum := 0;                   {Initialize variable.}

While Price <> 9999 do begin      {Test value of Counter.}

        Sum := Sum + Price                              {This statement Accumulates the total.}

            IF Price > Largest THEN

                    Largest = Price

            ENDIF

        ReadIn(Price); {Input the next item in the list.}


        End;    { Ends While loop when Price = 9999.}
    Writeln(' The largest value in the list is',Largest,'and the total is',Sum);
```

These steps are repeated until 9999

These statements select the largest value in the list

Example 3: Write a program that accepts the mark a student got in five subject areas. The program should output the average mark obtained by the student.

```
Counter := 0           {Initialize variable.}

Sum := 0

While Counter < 5 do begin                    {Test value of Counter.}
        Writeln('Enter the mark');

        ReadIn(mark);


    ReadIn(Mark);   {Input an item in the list.}

        Counter = Counter + 1;                    {Increments the Counter.}
```

```
          Sum  :=  Sum  +  Mark;                                    {Adds the marks.}


End;      {End While loop when Counter = 5.}

Average  :=  Sum/Counter;

Writeln('The average score obtained by the student is', Average);
```

2. For Statement

Repeats a group of statements a specified number of times.

Use this statement when you are told exactly how many repetitions there are.

Format	Terminology
For *counter* = *start* **To** *end* 　　　[Program *statements*] **End;{Endfor)**	*counter* 　　Numeric variable used as a loop counter. The variable can't be an array element or an element of a user-defined type. *start* 　　Initial value of *counter*. *end* 　　Final value of *counter*. *statements* 　　One or more statements between **For** and **End {Endfor}** that are executed the specified number of times

11 Comments:

Once the loop starts and all statements in the loop have executed, the *counter is increased by 1*. At this point, either the statements in the loop execute again (based on the same test that caused the loop to execute initially), or the loop is exited and execution continues with the statement following the **Next** statement.

Note Changing the value of *counter* while inside a loop can make it more difficult to read and debug your code.

Example 1: Write a program that accepts the mark a student got in five subject areas. The program should output the average mark obtained by the student.

```
Sum := 0    {Initialize variable.}

For Counter = 1 To 5  do begin            {Increment and Test value of Counter.}
```

Writeln('Enter the mark');

ReadIn(Mark)   {Input an item in the list.}

Sum := Sum + Mark   {Adds the marks.}

End;   {Ends **For** loop when Counter = 5.}

Average := Sum / counter

Writeln('The average score obtained by the student is',Average);

(Definite Loop) For Next Loop	In Pascal you can find the sum of the first 100 numbers like this: Sum := 0 For Counter := 1 to 100 do begin Sum = Sum + Counter End; Writeln('The sum of the first 100 numbers is', Sum);

While loop	In Pascal you can ask the name of students in a class in a while loop:
	
	Sum := 0
	
	ReadIn(number);
	
	While number <> 999 do begin
	
	   Sum := Sum + number
	
	   ReadIn(number);

	End; Writeln('The sum of the first 100 numbers is',Sum);
logical operators and statements	<> stands for not equal to, >= stands for greater or equal to Example of a logical statement (a sentence that is either true or false): FirstName = "John" and (Age <> 37 or Hobby = "Sailing)

1.   Write a program the calculates and prints the square of the first five integers.

Pseudocode:

12 Begin
    Counter = 0

    While counter < 5 **do**

            Square = counter ^ 2

            Counter = counter + 1

    Endwhile

    End

    Counter := 0; ' **Initialize variable.**

    While Counter < 20 do begin   ' **Test value of Counter.**

        square := Counter ^ 2;

        writeln('the square of ', Counter, 'is',square); ' **Outputs the square**

        Counter = Counter + 1;   ' **Increment Counter to go to the next integer.**

    End;   ' **End While loop when Counter => 20.**

2. **Write a program the reads a list of numbers terminated by an entry of -1 and prints the average and sum of the list.**

13 Begin

Sum = 0

Counter = 0

Print "Enter a number"

Read number

While number <> -1 do

    Sum = Sum + number

    Counter = Counter + 1

    Print "Enter a number"

    Read number

End while

Average = Sum / Counter

Print "The sum of the numbers entered is ", Sum

Print "The average of the numbers entered is ", Average

End

```
Sum := 0

Counter := 0

Readln(Number);

While Number <> -1 do begin

    Sum = Sum + Number;

    Counter = Counter + 1;

    Readln(Number);

End;

Average := Sum / Counter

Writeln('The sum of the'Counter + (
```

Information Technology

Programming Task

Topic: Loops;

    IF statements;

    Finding the maximum and minimum value in a list;

Maximum and minimum using the **FOR** loop:

1. Write a program that will accept a list of ten scores. The program should print out the maximum score.

2. Write a program that will accept a list of fifteen temperatures occurring during the month of May. The program should print out the minimum temperature for that month.

3. Write a program that will accept a list of twenty scores for the students in a class. The program should print out the maximum and minimum scores obtained by the students.

4. Write a program that will accept the price of fifteen items from supermarket and output the lowest price entered. The program should also output the total price of the items entered.

Maximum and minimum using the **WHILE** loop:

1. Write a program that will accept a list of scores terminated by an entry of 999. The program should print out the maximum score in the list.

2. Write a program that will accept a set of temperatures occurring during the month of May. The list is terminated by an entry of −1. The program should print out the minimum temperature for that month.

3. Write a program that will accept a set of scores terminated by an entry of 9999 for the students in a class. The program should print out the maximum and minimum scores obtained by the students.

4. Write a program that will accept a set price of items from supermarket and output the lowest price entered. The list is terminated when the price −1 is entered. The program should also output the total price of the items entered.

-

Information Technology

Programming

Topic: Totaling/summing a set of values;

Counting a set of values;

Counting a set of values for a given condition;

Loops;

1.   Write an algorithm that reads one hundred numbers and finds their sum.

2.   Write an algorithm to read a sequence of numbers terminated by 0 and print their sum. It should also print the amount of numbers entered.

3.   Write an algorithm to read a sequence of numbers terminated by 999. The algorithm should count and print the number of negative values (i.e. values less than zero) and the number of zero values.

4.   Write an algorithm to read the name and test scores for ten students. Each student does three tests. The algorithm must print the name of the student along with his/her average score.

5.   Write an algorithm to read a set of integers terminated by 0 and print their average.

6.   Write an algorithm to read a sequence of numbers terminated by 999 and print
a. the sum of the positive numbers
b. the sum of the negative numbers and
c. the product of the sums.

7.   The following data represent some sample scores obtained by students in a test:
5, 4, 7, 10. 0, 6, 0, 1, 9, 8, 999

999 is is a the dummy value which terminates the data. Write an algorithm to read any data in the above format and print the number of students scoring 0 and the number scoring 10.

8. Write an algorithm to read a sequence of fifteen numbers and pint the sum of all the even numbers.

9. Write an algorithm to read the names of a sequence of products and their price. The data terminates when a 0 price is entered for a product. Print the number of items purchased and the grand total.

14 Flow Charts

What is a flow chart?

Step-form and pseudocode program designs are both text-based, the statements are written. Flow charts are a graphical method of designing programs and once the rules are learned are very easy to draw. A well-drawn flow chart is also very easy to read since it basically uses just two symbols, two decision constructs. and two iteration constructs:

the sequence symbol,

the decision symbol,

the decision construct if ... then

the decision construct if ... then ... else

the repetition construct - repeat,

the repetition construct - while,

there are other symbols but the real work is depicted by the two symbols and the constructs. This shouldn't come as a surprise since in the step-form and pseudocode that is what you have been learning.

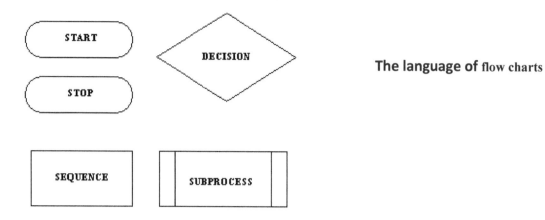

The language of flow charts

The major symbols are the DECISION (also known as selection) and the SEQUENCE (or process) symbols. The START and STOP symbols are called the terminals. The SUBPROCESS symbol is a variation on the sequence symbol. There are also connectors drawn between the symbols and you will see these used in the examples below. There is at least one other sequence symbol which is used to represent input/output processes but I think it is unnecessary so I don't use it.

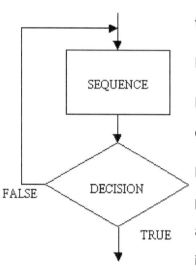

There are some important rules concerning the symbols and these rules apply also to other ways of stating algorithms:

Processes have only one entry point and one exit point.

Decisions have only one entry point, one TRUE exit point and one FALSE exit point.

Repeat loop. Note that the repeat loop has the process preceding the decision. This means that a repeat loop will always execute the process part at least once. This is an important point to remember because it may not be what you want to do. For instance assume you are a world power in control of an arsenal of nuclear weapons and have written a program to launch missiles in the event of an attack. Your program contains a loop which launches a missile each time you are struck by an enemy missile, for example:

REPEAT

 LAUNCH MISSILE

UNTIL ENEMY STOPS

Is a repeat loop a good idea in this case? Probably not since, if we assume you are not under attack and you run the program, the repeat loop executes the process at least once and you will probably start the next world war. A while loop would be a safer and more humane choice

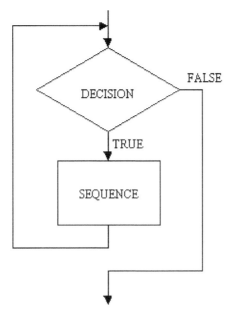

While loop. The while loop is basically the reverse of the repeat loop, the decision comes first, followed by the process. The while loop is usually written so that it iterates *while* the condition is true, the repeat iterates *until* the condition becomes true. An interesting question is: When should a repeat loop be used rather than a while loop? and vice-versa. The while loop should be used when it is possible that the process or processes which are in the scope of the decision (that is, in the loop) may not need to execute. For example assume you have a designed an air-conditioner controller program and the program turns on the compressor while the ambient temperature is above the desired temperature. A while loop is a good choice here since the ambient temperature may be at the desired level before the compressor part of the program is executed. If a repeat loop was used then the compressor would be turned on but it wouldn't be necessary. That would be wickedly ignorant of green sensitivities. A repeat loop would be a good candidate for the kind of situation in which a program needs to check for an external event at least once. For example: assume you have now written a program for a video cassete recorder and it has a menu for doing things like tuning TV channels, setting the date and time, programming events and so on. When the menu is displayed it is a QUIT option along with all the others, the VCR doesn't know which option will be chosen so it stays in the menu mode, that is repeats it, until QUIT is selected.

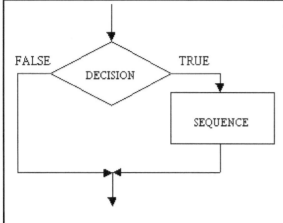

The IF ... THEN construct is shown here and is also known as the NULL ELSE, meaning that there is no ELSE part. I have use lines with arrow-heads (connectors) to indicate the flow of sequence. Although this is important in flow charts once you have gained some skill in using them and if you draw them carefully you will find that determining the sequence is straight forward. A typical rule is to use arrow-heads on connectors where flow direction may not be obvious.

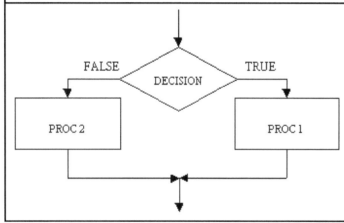

The IF ... THEN ... ELSE ... construct has a process at each branch of the decision symbol. The only difference here is that each value of the decision (TRUE/FALSE) has a process associated with it.

Using flow charts to design programs

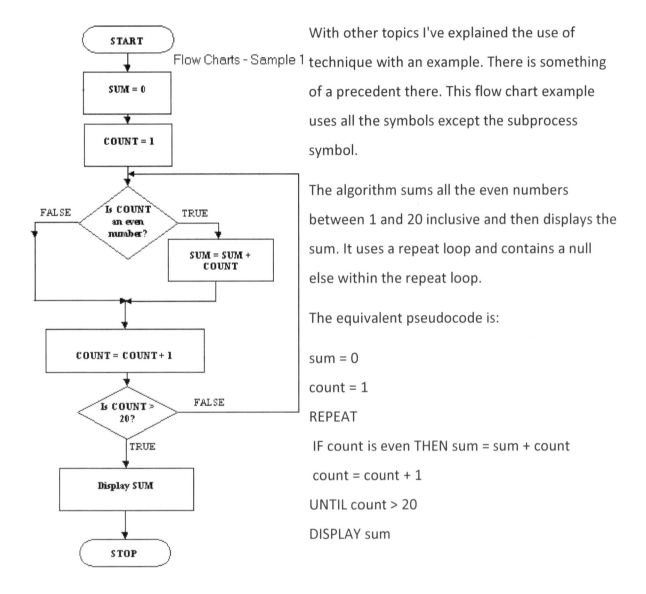

Flow Charts - Sample 1

With other topics I've explained the use of technique with an example. There is something of a precedent there. This flow chart example uses all the symbols except the subprocess symbol.

The algorithm sums all the even numbers between 1 and 20 inclusive and then displays the sum. It uses a repeat loop and contains a null else within the repeat loop.

The equivalent pseudocode is:

sum = 0

count = 1

REPEAT

 IF count is even THEN sum = sum + count

  count = count + 1

UNTIL count > 20

DISPLAY sum

You can see quite clearly from this example what the price of flow charting is. There is quite a bit of drawing to do in addition to writing the legend in the symbols. The pseudocode is quite simple by comparison so why would you use flow charts?

The major reasons are that the flow chart.

is easier to read more closely follows a standard, this is not the the case with pseudocode

probably lends itself more readily to computer-aided techniques of program design

Some rules for flow charts

Well-drawn flow charts are easy to read. What must you do to draw well-drawn flow charts? Here are a few rules:

Every flow chart has a START symbol and a STOP symbol

The flow of sequence is generally from the top of the page to the bottom of the page. This can vary with loops which need to flow back to an entry point.

Use arrow-heads on connectors where flow direction may not be obvious.

There is only one flow chart per page

A page should have a page number and a title

A flow chart on one page should not break and jump to another page

A flow chart should have no more than around 15 symbols (not including START and STOP)

Exercise 1

Now it's time for you to try your hand at designing a program using a flow chart.

Draw a flow chart and trace table for the following problem:

Fred sells bunches of flowers at the local shopping centre. One day Fred's boss, Joe, tells Fred that at any time during the day he (Joe) will need to know:

how many bunches of flowers have been sold

what was the value of the most expensive bunch sold

what was the value of the least expensive bunch sold

what is the average value of bunches sold

15 Flow charts and sub processes

There is one last topic to do while we are running hot on flow charts - dealing with subprocesses. Remember that when you studied pseudocode you learned about subprocesses and the benefits of using them.

The subprocess is useful because:

it provides a means of simplifying programs by making common processes available to a wide number of programs.

it permits the modularisation of complex programs.

it makes for more reliable programs since once it is shown that a process works then it can be made a subprocess and need not be tested again.

In flow charts subprocesses are also useful in dealing with the flow charting rule that a flow chart should have no more than 15 or so symbols on a page.

Here is an example of the use of subprocesses in flow charts:

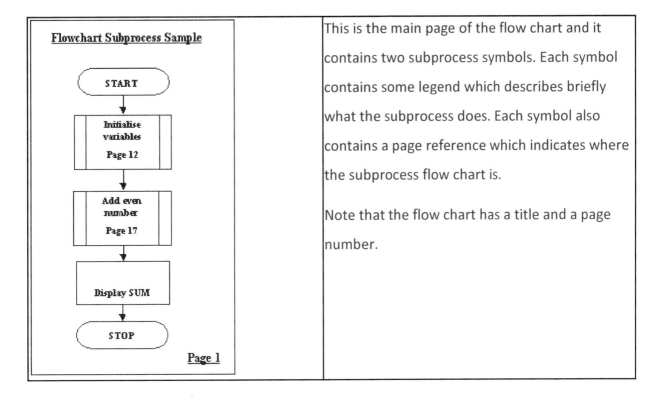

	This is the main page of the flow chart and it contains two subprocess symbols. Each symbol contains some legend which describes briefly what the subprocess does. Each symbol also contains a page reference which indicates where the subprocess flow chart is.
Flowchart Subprocess Sample START Initialise variables Page 12 Add even number Page 17 Display SUM STOP Page 1	Note that the flow chart has a title and a page number.

and here is page 12!

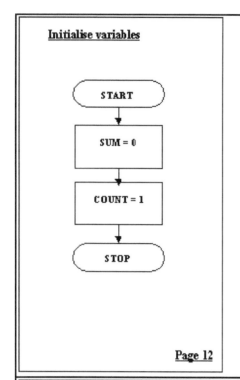

Initialise variables

START

SUM = 0

COUNT = 1

STOP

Page 12

The *Add even number* subprocess appears on its own page as indicated by the main flow chart on page 1.

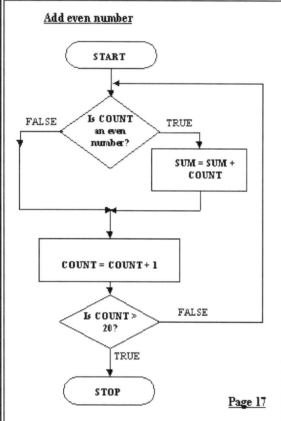

Add even number

START

Is COUNT an even number?

FALSE

TRUE → SUM = SUM + COUNT

COUNT = COUNT + 1

Is COUNT > 20?

FALSE

TRUE

STOP

Page 17

A subprocess flow chart can contain other subprocesses, there is no limit to how deeply these could be nested.

Exercise 2

With your answer for Exercise 1 modify the flow chart so that it has a main flow chart and shows each of the following as subprocess flow charts:

the initialisation of the variables

the process or processes for calculating how many bunches of flowers have been sold

the process or processes for calculating what was the value of the most expensive bunch sold

the process or processes for calculating what was the value of the least expensive bunch sold

the process or processes for calculating what is the average value of bunches sold

the display of all the result

Using nested loops in flow charts

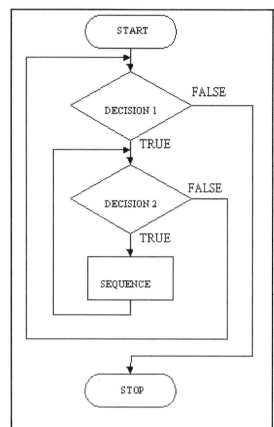

The nested while loop is shown here. This example is much simplified, it doesn't show any initialisation of either of the loops, the outer loop doesn't do any processing apart from the processing the inner loop, neither loop shows any statements which will lead to the termination of the loops.

Each single step through the outer loop will lead to the complete iteration of the innner loop. Assume that the outre loop counts through 10 steps and the inner loop through 100 steps. The sequence in the inner loop will be executed 10 * 100 times. Nested loops will do a lot of work.

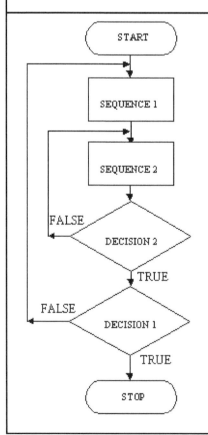

The repeat loop shown here, like the while loop example, is much simplified. It does show two processes, sequence 1 and sequence 2, one process in the outer loop and one process in the innner loop.

Like the while loop the nested repeat loop will see a great deal of work done. If the outer loop does a thousand iterations and the inner loops does a thousand iterations then sequence 2 will be executed 1000 * 1000 times.

Using multiway selection in flow charts

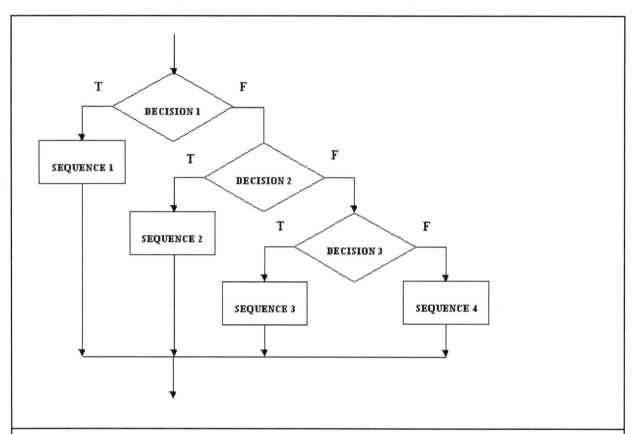

The flow chart form of multiway selection is shown here. You can see it how it shows quite clearly the notion of decisions nested within decisions.

If decision 1 is true then sequence 1 is executed and the multiway selection is finished. If decision 1 is false then decision 2 is tested, if this is true then sequence 2 is done and the multiway selection is finished. If decision 2 is false, you get the picture.

Review Task 1

Assume you have the following data stored somewhere:

Fred,Joan,Brian,Bert,Selie,Sue,Jack,Ng,Jacques,CLASS,Chris,Cheryl,Pam,Allan,CLASS,END

and it represents students in different classes.

Design a program using flow charts which:

reads the data and displays the names of the students in the class counts the number of students in each class

counts the number of classes

Review Task 2

Rewrite the nested loops and the multiway selection from above as pseudocode

Data Flow Diagrams:

A data flow diagram is a graphical representation showing how information flows through a system. It basically shows the system overview.

There are different levels of data flow diagrams. Each level indicates the amount of detail.

First, we draw a context level diagram (CLD). This shows the interaction between the system as a whole and the external agents. These external agents can either be data sources or data sinks. This context level diagram is then exploded into a 1st level DFD which shows the system in much more detail. The levels of DFD each shows how a system is divided into subsystems and how information flows from one subsystem to another.

There are certain notations which are used to depict processes. Let us see them one by one.

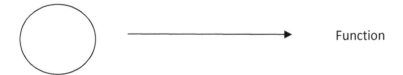

Function

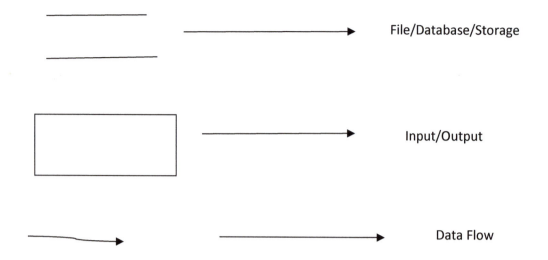

File/Database/Storage

Input/Output

Data Flow

Example of a data flow diagram:

Let us consider the library management system for example.

Context Level Diagram

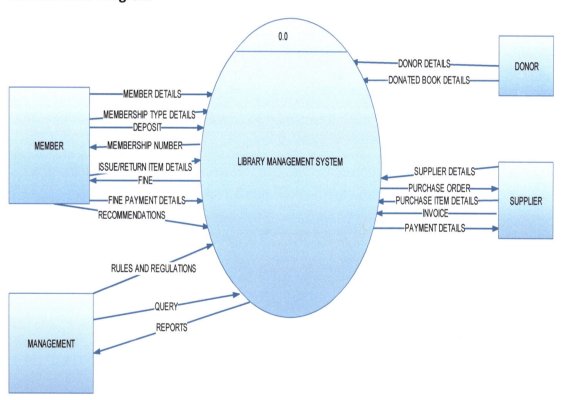

As we see, the system performs the following functions:

1. Maintains the member details

2. Handles management query and reports

3. Maintains supplier and payment details

4. Maintains membership type details

5. Donations/ Book Issue etc.

6. Book Purchase details

This CLD can be exploded into a first level DFD.

First Level DFD:

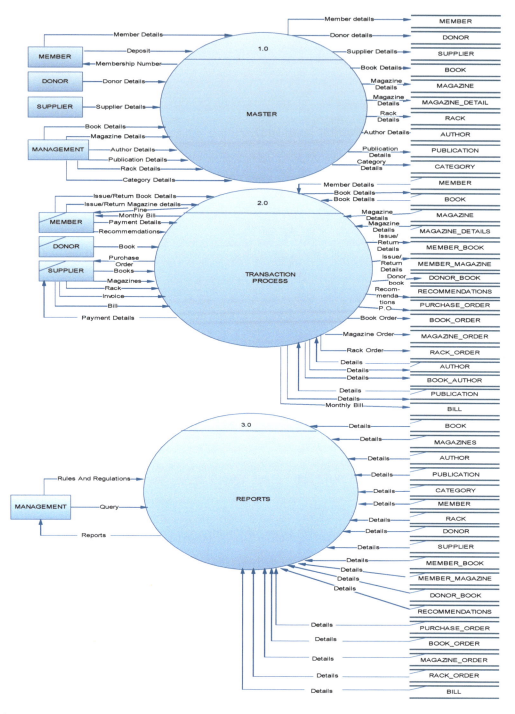

Case Study 2: Event Management System:

The system has the following functions:

1. Maintains Customer details

2. Maintains Event and Facility details

3. Maintains Employee information

4. Handles payments and enquiries

5. Reports and administration.

Context Level Diagram:

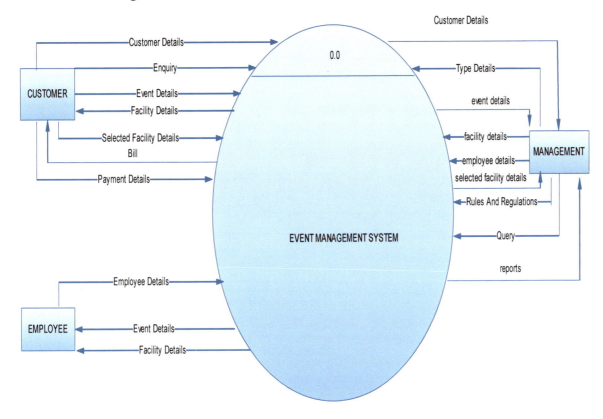

This CLD can be exploded into first level DFD.

MASTER DFD

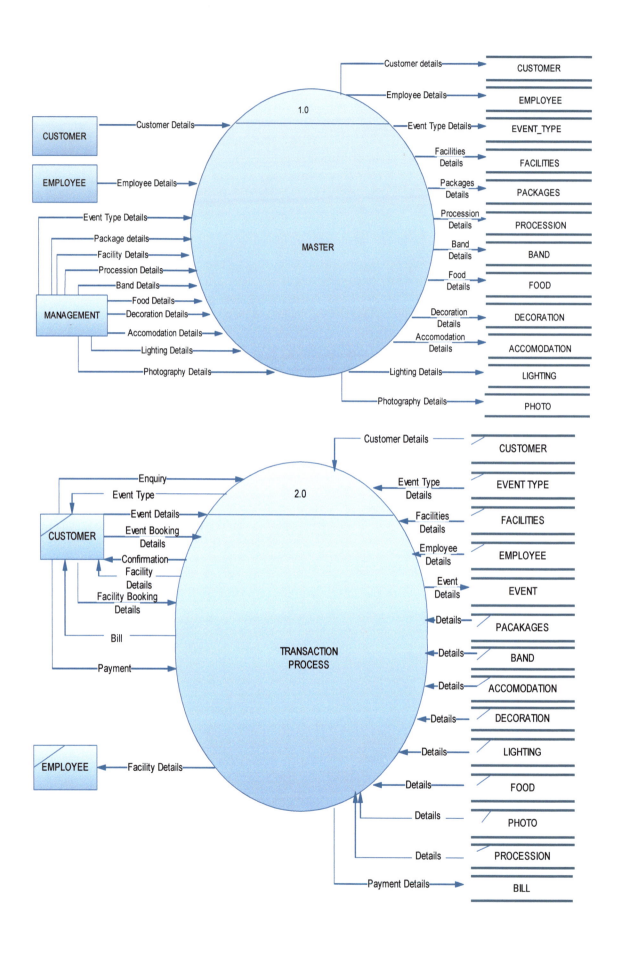

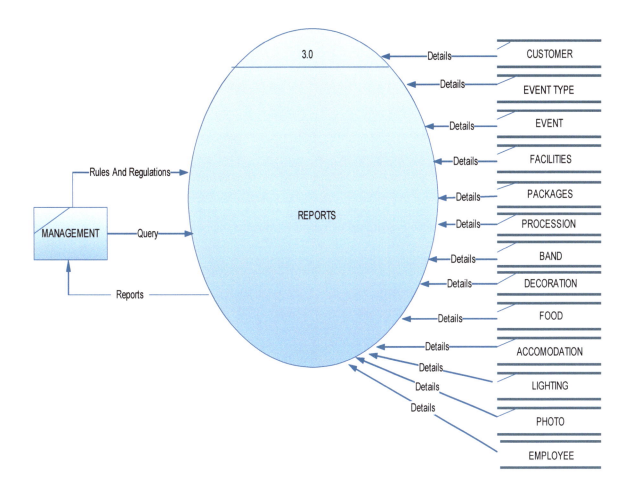

CASE STUDY: MASQUERADERS

Develop an algorithm or write pseudo code that accepts as input the names of an unspecified number of masqueraders who each have paid the full cost of their costume and the amount each has paid. A masquerader may have paid for a costume in any of the five sections in the band. The algorithm should determine the section in which a masquerader plays based on the amount he/she has paid for the costume. The algorithm should also determine the number of masqueraders who have paid for costumes in each section. The names of persons and the section for which they have paid should be printed. A listing of section and the total number of persons registered to play in each section should also be printed, along with the total amount of money paid in each section.

Solution:

Every algorithm follows a basic principle: IPO i.e. Input – Process – Output. Here, we already have the input data and the output required. Let us list them.

Input data:

1. Section's costume prices.

2. Amount a masquerader has paid.

Output Required:

1. To determine the section in which a masquerader will be put.

2. To determine the number of masqueraders in each section.

3. To print the list of names sectionwise.

4. To print section reports detailing the total number of persons, and total amount of money paid in each section.

Now we will write the pseudo code for the process.

Pseudo Code:

Initialize section1_cnt:=0, section2_cnt:=0, section3_cnt:=0, section4_cnt:=0, section5_cnt:=0.

Initialize section1_sum:=0, section2_sum:=0, section3_sum:=0, section4_sum:=0, section5_cnt:=0.

Initialize i: =1, j: =1.

Declare a 2-D array of characters member.

Do

While (j <2) do

Input member name.

Input member amount.

member [i][j]:=name.

if (j=1) then begin

      if (amount = 160) then begin

```
                section1_cnt:=section1_cnt + 1

                member [i][j]:='1'

                section1_sum:=section1_sum + 1

                Print member[i][j]

        end

        if (amount = 220) then begin

                section2_cnt:=section2_cnt + 1

                member [i][j]:='2'

                section2_sum:=section2_sum + 1

                Print member[i][j]

        end

    .   if (amount = 280) then begin

                section3_cnt:=section3_cnt + 1

                member [i][j]:='3'

                section3_sum:=section3_sum + 1

                Print member[i][j]

        end

        if (amount = 350) then begin

                section4_cnt:=section4_cnt + 1

                member [i][j]:='4'

                section4_sum:=section4_sum + 1

                Print member[i][j]

        end

        if (amount = 425) then begin

                section5_cnt:=section5_cnt + 1

                member [i][j]:='5'

                section5_sum:=section5_sum + 1
```

```
                    Print member[i][j]
        end
End
j:=j+1
End While.
i:=i+1
j:=1
Input choice.
While choice = "yes" or choice = "yes"
Print "--------------------SECTION AND COUNT-------------------------"
Print '1', section1_cnt
Print '2', section2_cnt
Print '3', section3_cnt
Print '4', section4_cnt
Print '5', section 5_cnt
For k:=1, k<=i; k++ do
For j:=1, j<=2; j++ do
        Print member [k][j];
End For
End For
Print '1', section1_cnt, section1_sum
Print '2', section2_cnt, section2_sum
Print '3', section3_cnt, section3_ sum
Print '4', section4_cnt, section4_sum
Print '5', section 5_cnt, section5_sum
End.
```

Summary:

In this chapter we studied:

- Algorithmic way of problem solving
- Various elements of an algorithm
- Narratives, pseudocode and flowchart being the different ways of representing an algorithm
- The different control structures available for algorithm implementation
- Data flow diagrams and how to use them.

Section – 3: Program Implementation using Pascal

Chapter Objectives:

In this chapter, we will learn:

- How to use programming languages to communicate with the computer.
- About the **generations of programming lan**guages.
- About translators and compilers.
- The steps in implementing a program.
- About the different elements of the PASCAL language like data types, arrays, files, searching and sorting, variables and constants.

Programming Languages

Programming languages are how we build softwares which in turn are used to communicate with the computer system. Studying programming languages help us write and understand what we commonly know as programs.

What is a program?

A program is a set of instructions written in a format which follows the semantics of a prescribed computer language.

Whenever a program is executed, the computer system will carry out the tasks which it has been asked to perform. To program a computer is to tell it what to do.

Remember: A computer is a human's slave. Humans command, the computer obeys. This has always been the paradigm.

The person who writes a program is known as a programmer. A programmer needs to have certain qualities in order to be efficient and successful. They are:

1. He/she must be curious to know more about the language and willing to go into the depth.

2. He/she needs to come up with creative solutions in case a situation arrives.

3. He/she needs to be bold in front of the mammoth tasks which will inevitably arise as the programmer learns more.

4. He/she needs to be humble. A programmer needs to know that writing a program is difficult. He/she should accept that fact.

5. He/she must be stubborn. If any error persists, the programmer should not easily give up.

6. He/she should have a logical mind. The ability to reason is a quality which is looked for the most in programmers.

Building a program involves the following steps:

1. The problem is discovered first.

2. A step by step solution is found. In other words, an algorithm is developed.

3. Translate the algorithm into a program written in a suitable computer programming language.

4. Test the program on a computer.

5. If test reveals errors then fix it or improve solution.

6. Write user documentation.

What does a good program look like?

- It should be **easy to use** with limited training and support.
- It should be **robust** to cope with errors without producing wrong results or stopping.
- It should be **flexible** so it can be easily customised for use in a specific situation.
- It should be **reliable** so it won't stop due to design faults.
- It should be **portable** so it can be used on different computer hardware.
- It should be **easily maintained** so errors can be corrected, new modules can be introduced, and performance can be enhanced.

Programming languages are classified into two categories:

1. High Level Languages: High level languages are very close to the English language and hence easily understandable. They can be easily debugged and rendered error-free.

2. Low Level Languages: They are machine level code and hence understood properly only by the computer system. They are tough to debug.

Depending upon the time in which the language was invented, programming languages have been classified into generations.

Review Questions:

1. Define programming language.

2. What is a program? Why is the program so important?

3. Broadly classify programming languages.

4. What are the characteristics of a good programmer?

5. The person who writes a program is called a _____. (Fill in the blank)

6. Mention the characteristics of a good program.

Programming Language Generations:

Programming instructions are written in accordance with a **programming language** e.g. Visual Basic. Each programming language has its own **rules** and **commands**. A **command** is a word, which tells the computer to perform a specific action. Programming languages are classified as:-

    i.   Machine language.
    ii.   Assembly language.
    iii.   High-level language.
    iv.   Fourth generation languages.

(a)   Machine language (First generation language) :-
A microprocessor can understand only instructions represented by binary digits--machine language. Any instructions issued to a machine, either by the user or a program, must be converted to machine language for execution.

Characteristics of Machine Language:

- Is written using **0s** and **1s** only.
- Programs are **tedious** to write in this language and it is therefore easy for the programr to make mistakes.
- These programs are machine dependent i.e. they may not work on computers other than those for which they were written.
- Programs execute **faster** than programs written in other languages.
- The machine understands this language. Therefore no translation is required as is the case with other languages.

(b)   Assembly language (Second generation language) :-
A series of mnemonic statements that can be "assembled" (translated) into low-level machine language using a program called an assembler. This language is fast and efficient, but very difficult to read or write.

Characteristics:

- Is written using **short codes** (mnemonics) e.g. **ADD, STO, SUB**.

- Programs are machine dependent i.e. they may not work on computers that they were not specifically written for.
- Programmers have to focus on both machine and software.
- Programs do not execute as fast as machine language programs.
- Translation to machine code is required.

(c)   High-level language(s) (Third generation language) :-
Is a machine-independent, procedural language that uses human words and symbols to program diverse computer systems e.g. **Cobol, Fortran**, **Pascal, Basic, C**

Characteristics of High Level Language:

- Is **not machine dependent.**
- Use **English like statements.**
- Is **easier** to write than earlier generation languages.
- Were developed with particular objectives in mind:
    - **Cobol** was developed for processing large volumes of data e.g. Billing, accounts, inventory.
    - **Fortran** was developed for solving complex mathematical problems.
    - **Pascal** was developed to assist students in understanding programming.
    - **Basic** was developed for solving math and business problems.
    - **C** was developed for writing operating systems and business software.

(d)   High-level language(s) - Fourth generation language (4GL) :-
- A programming language that contains constructs that allow a programr to express system logic to a computer system in a manner that is closer to the natural language that he/she uses than earlier generation computer languages.
  One statement in a fourth generation language **such as Progress** typically corresponds to many lines of code in a third generation language **such as C, Cobol or Fortran**.

- Generally refers to a group of high level languages used primarily for the manipulation of data bases. 4GL languages have a syntax mimicking the English language and operate on sets or subsets of data rather than on single elements as do most conventional languages (such as FORTRAN or PASCAL).

(e)   Fifth Generation Language:-

This is commonly abbreviated as 5GL. This language is based on solving problems using the constraints given to a program rather than using an algorithm. This generation of programming languages are designed to let the computer system solve the problem on its own i.e. without a programmer. These languages are mainly used in the field of artificial intelligence and expert systems which heavily use the concept of natural language. Examples include Prolog, OPS5, and Mercury.

Review Questions:

1. Classify programming languages by generation.

2. Write a note about:

(i) First Generation

(ii) Second Generation

(iii) Third Generation

(iv) Fourth Generation

3. Describe the Fifth generation of programming languages.

Translators

Translation languages convert program commands into machine code.There are two main types of translation languages. These are:

- o Interpreters
- o Compilers

Interpreters convert each instruction into machine code, and then carry them out while compilers convert the whole program into machine code before carrying the instructions out. The following diagram shows the relationship among the translators

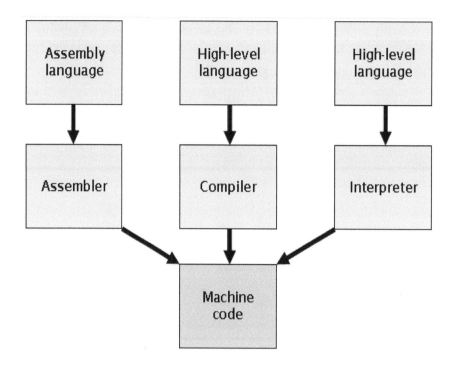

Steps in Implementing a Program

Implementing a program involves certain steps.

1. Creating the source code: Source code is the program in question. This is written in a computer language understood by the programmer.

2. Compiling the source code: Once the source code is written completely, we need to compile it. Compilation results in an executable code.

3. Linking: This function is carried out by a system software known as linker. The linker takes the object files which are generated by the compiler and combine them into a single executable file.

4. Executing: The execution of the program takes place after the linker creates the necessary executable file.

5. Maintaining: Errors, both compile time and runtime, need to be corrected and debugged. The code needs to be continuously monitored in order to ensure that the correct output is displayed to the user.

Some Programming Terminologies

testing	Efforts made to examine if a program is grammatically correct (no syntax errors), does what was intended (no logical errors), and runs well (no runtime errors).
debugging	The detection, location and correction of program errors (bugs).
logical error	An error in the design of the program. The program may be grammatically correct, but it is not doing what you intended it to do.
syntax error	An incorrect use of the rules that construct legal program statements. A grammatical mistake.
runtime error	Error that is first detected when the program is run. Examples: attempt to divide by zero, overflow.
test data	Data used to test a program. It may be wise to use normal, extreme and illegal data for testing.
Dry Run	Testing process where a scenario of a possible failure is intentionally created.

Review Questions:

1. Write a note on translators.

2. What do you mean by a compiler?

3. Define the following terms:

a. Test data

b. Dry Run

c. Debugging

4. Enumerate the steps in implementing a program.

PROGRAMMING IN PASCAL

We will be using the software 'Lazarus' for executing the programs. Lazarus is an open source integrated development IDE for executing programs based on the PASCAL programming language.

PASCAL is a procedural programming language which was designed in 1969 and published in 1970 by Niklaus Wirth. This language intends to encourage good programming practices using structured programming and data structuring.

An object oriented version of this language has also been developed, which we know as Object Pascal. This was developed in the year 1985.

The Pascal compiler is open source and is free for download. The software 'Lazarus' which we will be using for executing our Pascal programs run on the Free Pascal compiler. Here is what the default Free Pascal IDE looks like.

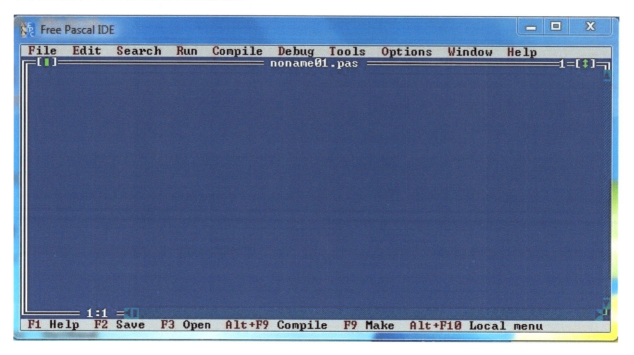

This is the basic software to execute Pascal programs. You can use this for executing the Pascal programs we will be learning soon.

Lazarus is a development software which allows both command line programming and graphics driven programming. If we click the Lazarus icon from our installation directory, we get the following screen.

We will not be using form based programming in this chapter. So we will keep ourselves to the text mode.

Click on the File menu and then click on new. You should get the following screen.

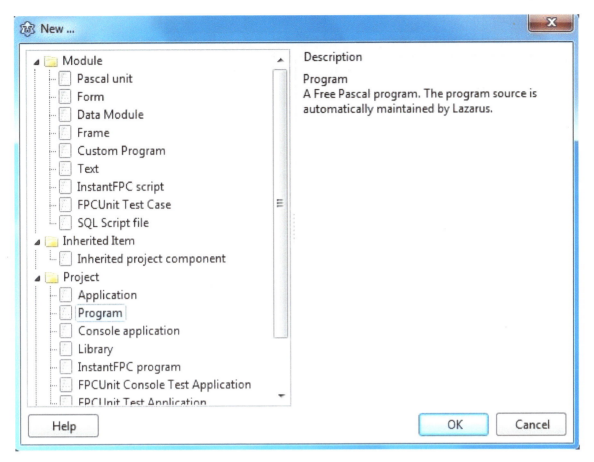

Click on the Program under the Project heading. You should get the following screen.

```
1    program Project1;
.
.    {$mode objfpc}{$H+}
.
5    uses
.      {$IFDEF UNIX}{$IFDEF UseCThreads}
.      cthreads,
.      {$ENDIF}{$ENDIF}
.      Classes
10     { you can add units after this };
.
12   begin    |
.    end.
14
```

12: 9   INS   project1.lpr

Pascal Editor and Library

This is the source editor where we will write our code.

Now let us write some code to see whether the program works.

Sample snippet:

> Writeln ('This is Free Pascal and Lazarus');
>
> Writeln ('Press Enter key to close');
>
> Readln;

1. Every line ends with a semicolon.

2. Writeln function is used to display output.

3. Readln function is used to read the input.

Now, we insert this snippet into our main program between the begin and end statements. This is shown below:

```
Source Editor                                    _ □ X

project1.lpr

 1  program project1;
    .
    .  {$mode objfpc}{$H+}
    .
 5  uses
    .    {$IFDEF UNIX}{$IFDEF UseCThreads}
    .    cthreads,
    .    {$ENDIF}{$ENDIF}
    .    Classes
10    { you can add units after this };
    .
    . begin
    .    Writeln('This is Free Pascal and Lazarus');
    .    Writeln('Press Enter key to close');
15    Readln;
16  end.              |
17

 ◄   III                                          ►

 16: 16                 INS     C:\Users\Admin\Documents\project1.lpr
```

Save this as project1.lpr.

To compile this file, click on Run, and then click on Compile. Alternatively, we could use the keyboard function CTRL + F9.

We get the following message if the program does not give compilation errors.

Once compiled, we execute it. Click on Run menu again and then again, click on the Run menu item. Alternatively, press the F9 key.

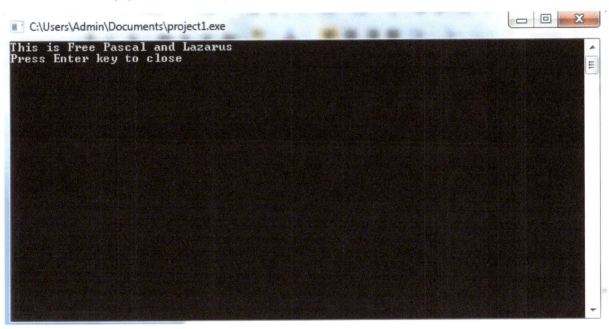

Pressing the Enter key will result in termination of the program. The following screen will be shown.

We can choose either option. If we click the button to the right, this message will not be shown again.

Now in the previous program, we will change the line

Writeln ('This is Free Pascal and Lazarus');

To

Writeln ('This is a number:', 15);

Now let us see what the output will be.

Now again, we will change the previous line to this one.

Code:

Writeln ('This is a number:', 7 + 5);

The output is shown below:

As we see, '+' is the addition operator.

Next, we check for multiplication. '*' is the operator we use for multiplication.

Code:

*Writeln ('This is a number:', 7 * 6);*

Now, the output is shown below.

Let us now see what happens if you put in this line.

Code:

Writeln ('This is a number:', 5.4);

The output is shown below:

Now we will learn how to display multiple outputs in a single line.

Replace the original line with this one:

Code:

Writeln ('One, Two, Three:', 1, 2, 3);

Let us now see the output:

Now we will write a sentence.

Code:

*Writeln ('10 * 3 :', 10 * 3);*

Output:

10 * 3 : 30

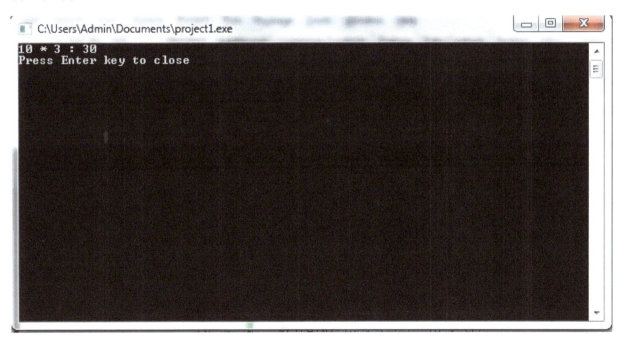

Pascal Programs

Variables and Constants:

Variables and constants form a key part of any programming language. Pascal is no exception. One of the most fundamental requirements of a programming language is the ability to assign values to variables. Variables are symbolic names that refer to a storage location where the value of the variable is stored. It is called a variable because the value that it contains can be changed while the program is executing. To help programmers write robust code, variables are assigned types so that the value in the variable is interpreted in the correct fashion. Variables are assigned values by the use of expressions. Both of these topics are covered next.

Variables are like data containers. For instance, let us say we have a variable named X. We assign a value, say 7, to it. X=7 means that the variable X contains the value 7.

Variables in Pascal are declared before the 'begin' statement. They are prefixed using the 'var' keyword. Any lines following this keyword will indicate the declaration of variables.

Data Types
Variable Types

The types of values that can be contained in a variable by in large belong to a few basic groups. A value can represent either a logical, numeric or character value. The numeric value is further distinguished between an integer and a floating-point value. Each of the variable types can be grouped into what is called an array or table. An array is a collection of values, all of the same type that represent multiple instances of a variable. A special case is a constant, which is a type of variable whose value never changes. Categorizing a constant as a variable type is a misnomer but for convenience sake it is defined this way.

Logical

Logical variables contain Boolean values. A Boolean value indicates whether something is true or false. Therefore a variable that is a logical type can only contain one of two values, either true or false. In the expression section we will see how multiple logical variables can be operated upon to produce a new true or false value.

Examples:

Boolean logicalvar; //declaring the variable named logicalvar to be of type Boolean logicalvar := 1; //a variable assignment, typically 1 means true

logicalvar := 0; //a variable assignment, typically 0 means false

More variable assignment, some language have a keyword for true and false and the actual value that codes the true and false are hidden from the programmer.

logicalvar := true;

logicalvar := false;

Numeric

Numeric variables contain values that represent numbers. These numbers can either be integer or floating-point values. Integer values are whole numbers; they do not have a decimal point. Floating-point values do have a decimal point and thus can represent fractional parts of a number like 23.341. Each of these two basic types of numbers can use different amounts of memory to contain their values. The amount of memory that is reserved for the numbers will affect the range of values the number can accurately represent. Recall from the Data Representation Size Units section that the number of bits determines all the possible values that are contained within a size unit.

Integer

Integer values are typically defined to use different amounts of memory. The motivation for this is conserve memory. If the range of possible values that the numeric integer variable is to contain can be stored in that amount of memory, then use that type so that memory is not wasted.

Let us see a sample code declaring an integer.

Code:

```
Program: firstvar;
{$mode objfpc}{$H+}
Uses
        {$IFDEF UNIX }{$IFDEF UseCThreads}
        Cthreads,
        {$ENDIF}{$ENDIF}
        Classes
```

```
        { you can add units after this };
Var
        X: Integer;
Begin
        X: = 12;
        Writeln (X * 2);
        Writeln ('Press enter key to close.');
        Readln;
End
```

Output:

We will get 24 as the output.

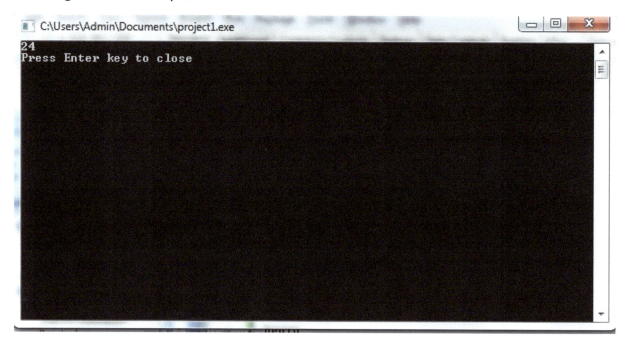

One can declare two variables in the same line provided they are of the same data type.

Code:

```
Var
        X,  Y: Integer;
Begin
        X:=10;
        Y:=15;
        Writeln (x * y);
        Writeln ('Press enter key to close');
        Readln;
End
```

Output:

The output of this code will be 150.

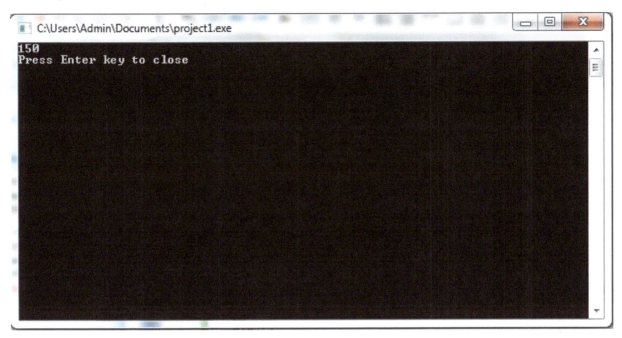

Real

Real values are typically defined to use different amounts of memory. The motivation for this is to conserve memory. If the range of possible values that the numeric floating-point variable is to contain can be stored in that amount of memory, then use that type so that memory is not wasted. Because floating-point numbers record the value to the left and the right of the decimal point, providing greater precision for very small numbers (close to zero) also motivates the different sizes. Typical floating-point types are Float (single) or Double.

Float (single)

Float or single, so named because of the single precision of the floating-point numbers is typically defined to be 32 bits. Depending on the scheme used to encode the floating-point number the range of values is determined. Floating-point numbers are inherently signed so the range is always a plus/minus (+/-) range. The IEEE 754 floating-point standard yields a range of +/-1.4E-45 to +/-3.4028235E+38. This range is in scientific notation.

Here is the code snippet which shows how to use this data type.

Code:

```
Var:
X: Single;
Begin
        X:=2.8;
        Writeln ('John Doe stays ',x,' kms from here.');
        Writeln('Press enter key to close.');
        Readln
End
```

Here is the output for this code:

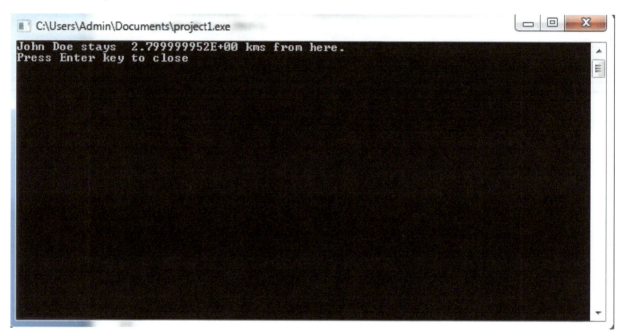

Double

Double, more aptly name because it provides double the precision of float (single) is typically defined to be 64 bits. Again, depending on the scheme used to encode the floating-point number the range of values is determined. Floating-point numbers are inherently signed so the range is always a plus/minus (+/-) range. The IEEE 754 floating-point standard yields a range of +/-4.9E-324 to +/-1.7976931348623157E+308. This range is in scientific notation.

Scientific Notation

This notation is a short-hand way of representing floating-point numbers. To convert from scientific notation to standard decimal notation take the number on the left of the E and multiply it by ten (10) raised to the power of the number of the right of E. If the number to the right of E is negative then the decimal value will have many digits to the right of the decimal point. If the number to the right of E is positive then the decimal value will have many digits to the left of the decimal point. The number of zeros to place on the left or right (depending on the sign) of the decimal point is one less than the number to the right of E, the number that is raised to the power of ten (10).

For Example,

+1.4E-45 is 0.0000 (for 44 zeros)14

-1.4E-45 is –0.0000 (for 44 zeros)14

+3.4028235E+38 is 34028235 (another 37 zeros).0

-3.4028235E+38 is -34028235 (another 37 zeros).0

Character

Character variables contain values that represent characters. This class of variable type can either be a single character or a series ("string") of characters. The typical names for these two character types are char and string.

Char

A char is defined to contain a single character. The amount of memory (number of bits, bytes) that a character uses is depended on the encoding scheme used. The ASCII character take 8 bits, 1 byte. Whereas, Unicode characters take 16 bits, 2 bytes.

Here is a code snippet which shows how to declare and use character variables

Code:

```
Var
        C: Char;
Begin
```

```
C:= 'B';
Writeln ('My first letter is:', C);
Writeln ('Press enter key to close:');
Readln;
End
```

Here is the output:

String

A string is defined to contain a sequence of individual characters. The amount of memory used depends on how much memory is required for each character and how many characters are in the string. Strings are not fixed lengths like all the other type discussed so far and therefore the computer cannot directly process strings. A language must have some system of storing and managing strings.

In all our above programs, we have assigned values to our variables. However, most practical scenarios dictate that the software be interactive and flexible. Notice that in all the programs we have written so far, there is hardly any interaction with the user, except for the 'enter key scenario'. Now, we are going to change that.

Code:

Var

```
        X: Integer;
Begin

        Write ('Please input any number:');
        Readln (x);
        Writeln ('You have entered:', x);
        Writeln ('Press Enter key to close');
        Readln;
End
```

Here, the value is input by the user. Let us see what output this code generates.

First, it prompts the user to input a number as shown below.

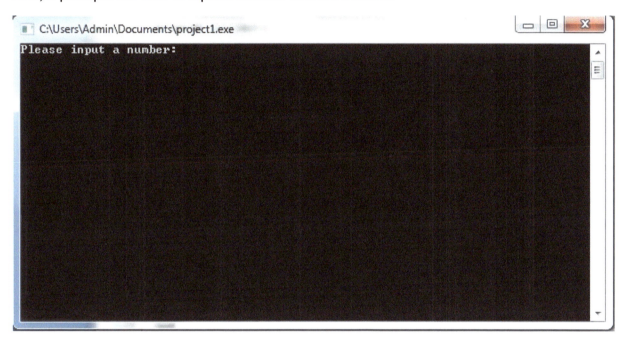

After the user inputs data and presses 'Enter', we get the output.

Until now, we have seen very simple programs. Let us notch the complexity up a bit. Let us now display a multiplication table of a number we will input through the command line prompt. The code is shown in the figure below:

Code:

```
1    program project1;

.    {$mode objfpc}{$H+}

5    uses
     {$IFDEF UNIX}{$IFDEF UseCThreads}
     cthreads,
     {$ENDIF}{$ENDIF}
     Classes
10   { you can add units after this };
     var

.    x:Integer;
.    begin
15   Write('Please input a number:');
.    Readln(x);
.    Writeln(x,' * 1 = ', x*1);
18   Writeln(x,' * 2 = ', x*2);
.    Writeln(x,' * 3 = ', x*3);
20   Writeln(x,' * 4 = ', x*4);
.    Writeln(x,' * 5 = ', x*5);
.    Writeln(x,' * 6 = ', x*6);
.    Writeln(x,' * 7 = ', x*7);
.    Writeln(x,' * 8 = ', x*8);
25   Writeln(x,' * 9 = ', x*9);
.    Writeln(x,' * 10 = ', x*10);
.    Writeln(x,' * 11 = ', x*11);
.    Writeln(x,' * 12 = ', x*12);
.    Writeln('Press enter key to close');
30   Readln;


.    end.
34
```

Implementing Pascal Code
Code Listing:

```pascal
program projectmul;

{$mode objfpc}{$H+}
uses
  {$IFDEF UNIX}{$IFDEF UseCThreads}
  cthreads,
  {$ENDIF}{$ENDIF}
  Classes
  { you can add units after this };
var
x:Integer;
begin
Write('Please input a number:');
Readln(x);
Writeln(x,' * 1 = ', x*1);
Writeln(x,' * 2 = ', x*2);
Writeln(x,' * 3 = ', x*3);
Writeln(x,' * 4 = ', x*4);
Writeln(x,' * 5 = ', x*5);
Writeln(x,' * 6 = ', x*6);
Writeln(x,' * 7 = ', x*7);
Writeln(x,' * 8 = ', x*8);
Writeln(x,' * 9 = ', x*9);
Writeln(x,' * 10 = ', x*10);
Writeln(x,' * 11 = ', x*11);
Writeln(x,' * 12 = ', x*12);
Writeln('Press enter key to close');
Readln;
end.
```

Variables and constants enclosed within single quotation marks are written as is. However, when they are written without them, they are evaluated first and then written as values. For example:

```pascal
Writeln ('5 * 3');
```

The output of this line of code is: 5 * 3.

```pascal
Writeln (5 * 3);
```

The output of this line of code is: 15.

Now that we are done with variables, let us perform some arithmetic operations on them. Let us look at the following code snippet which inputs two numbers, performs addition, subtraction, multiplication, and division on them, and then prints the results.

Code:

```
Var
X, Y: Integer;
Resadd: Integer;
Ressub: Integer;
Resmul: Integer;
Resdiv: Single;
Begin
        Write ('Input a number:');
        Readln (X);
        Write ('Input another number:');
        Readln (Y);

        Resadd:= X + Y;
        Writeln (x, ' + ', y, ' = ', Resadd);
        Ressub:= X-Y;
        Resmul:= X * Y;
        Resdiv:= X / Y;
        Writeln (x, ' – ', y, ' = ', Ressub);
        Writeln (x, ' * ', y, ' = ', Resmul);
        Writeln (x, ' / ', y, ' = ', Resdiv);
        Writeln ('Press enter key to close:');
        Readln;
End
```

Let us now see the output of this code:

```
C:\Users\Admin\Documents\project1.exe

Input a number:6
Input another number:7
6+ 7 = 13
6 ГÇô 7 = -1
6 * 7 = 42
6 / 7 =  8.571428657E-01
Press enter key to close
```

Conditional Branching

Whatever programs we have dealt with so far, they follow the tenets of the sequence control structure. This means every statement is executed line after line. However, this will not work for every practical situation. There may come a time where we would want the software to make some decisions for us. This is where we come to the conditional control structure.

The conditional control structure allows the program execution to branch depending on how the conditional statements evaluate. As in every other programming language, PASCAL provides us with the 'IF' condition statement.

The 'IF' condition statement is usually followed by an 'else' statement should there be some message for the user if the condition evaluates to false.

Let us look at a sample program to show how the 'IF..Else' construct works.

Code:

```
Var
      Somevar: Integer;
Begin
      Write ('Please enter a value:');
      Readln (Somevar);
      If Somevar * 2 = 30 then
            Writeln ('The number you have entered is 15.')
      Else

            Writeln ('The number you have entered is not 15.');
      Writeln ('Press enter key to close.');
      Readln;
```

Let us now see what the output of this code looks like

First, let us try the input with the correct number, meaning let us now see how it branches to the statement following the evaluation of the condition to true.

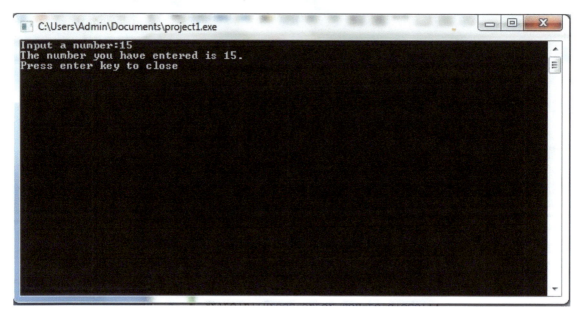

Now let us see what happens if the condition evaluates to false.

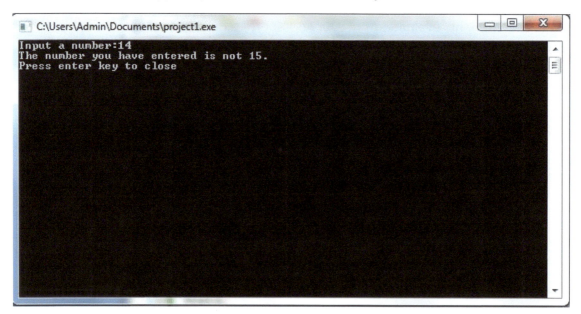

We can have multiple conditions in a program. This is shown in the following code.

Code:

Var
X: Integer;
Begin
Write ('Input a number:');
Readln (x);
*If x * 2 = 30 then*
Writeln ('number you have entered is 15.')
Else
*If x * 3 = 30 then*
Writeln ('number you have entered is 10.')
Else
Writeln ('number you have entered is neither 15 nor 10.');
Writeln ('press enter key to close.');
Readln;
End

Let us now see how this goes.

Scenario 1: First condition evaluates to true.

The message corresponding to this conditional statement is displayed to the user and then control skips to the end of the construct.

The output is shown below:

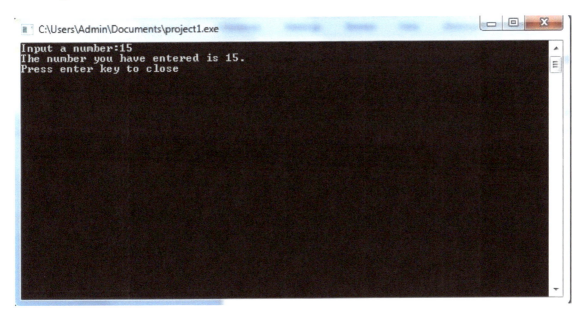

If this condition evaluates to false, it goes to the else part. Now here, the compiler sees that there is another 'if' condition. This condition sees whether the input number when multiplied by 3 gives the result 30. This means the input number must be 10.

So we come to Scenario 2:

Scenario 2: Second condition evaluates to true.

The message corresponding to this 'If' condition is displayed to the user and then the control skips to the end of the program.

The output is shown below.

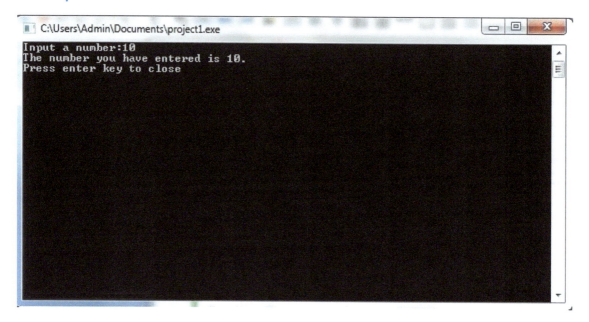

If this condition evaluates to false, it goes to the else part. Here the compiler now knows that the number x is neither 15 nor 10. This means both the conditions have now evaluated to false. So, it displays the message corresponding to the else part and skips to the end of the program.

Let us now see the output.

There may be situations where we would need to combine two conditions within a single 'if' condition. Here we may come to appreciate the use of logical operators.

Logical operators which we commonly use are 'AND' and 'OR'. The condition using 'AND' as logical operator evaluates to true if and only both the conditions evaluate to true. Let us now see the truth table for this.

Truth Table for 'AND':

Condition 1	Condition 2	1 And 2
True	True	True
True	False	False
False	True	False
False	False	False

This truth table is for only two conditions. However, there may be multiple conditions in the 'If' condition.

The theorem is that if there are 'n' conditions, there are 2^n entries in the truth table. This applies for every logical operator except 'NOT'.

In case of 'AND', it may suffice to know that the condition using this operator evaluates to true if and only if all the conditions evaluate to true. Let us now see a program incorporating this logical operator.

Code:

```
Var
X: Integer;
Begin
Writeln ('Input a number:');
Readln(X);
If (X = 5) and (X + 2 = 7) then
Writeln ('You have input correct number.')
Else
Writeln ('You are forbidden to cross the door.');
Writeln ('Press enter key to close.');
Readln;
End
```

Here are the outputs.

Scenario 1: Both conditions are evaluated to true

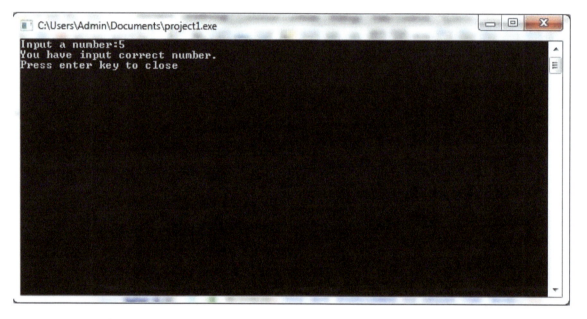

Scenario 2: Both conditions or either one evaluates to false

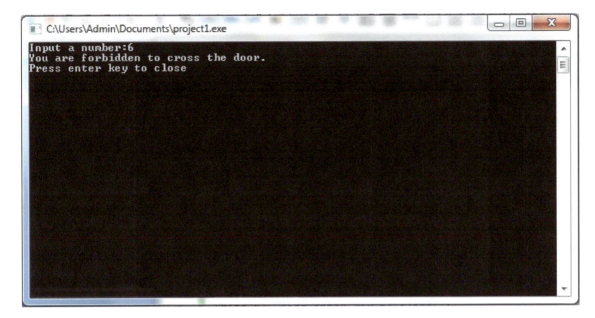

Notice that in the above program, both the conditions have to evaluate to false. There is no scenario where

Code:

```
Var
X, Y: Integer;
Begin
Readln(x);
Readln(y);
If (x=8) and (y=9) then
Writeln ('You may pass.');
Else
Writeln ('You cannot pass.');
Writeln ('press enter key to pass.');
end
```

The output of this program is:

Both conditions evaluate to true:

Both conditions evaluate to false or atleast one condition evaluates to false:

An important thing to note is that there can be multiple 'if...then...else' in a program. However, as we incorporate more of this construct, the complexity becomes higher and the program is not so easily readable. To rectify this issue, PASCAL provides us with the Case...Of construct.

This is another method for conditional branching.

For instance, we will now consider the following program.

Menus

Code:

```
Var
Meal: byte;
Begin
Writeln ('Welcome to the shoe shop. Please select your brand.');
Writeln ('1. Liberty');
Writeln ('2. Nike');
Writeln ('3. Reebok');
Writeln ('4. Adidas');
Writeln ;
Write ('Please enter your selection:');
Readln (Meal);
```

Case Meal of
1: writeln ('You have ordered Liberty shoes.');
2: writeln ('You have ordered Nike shoes.');
3: writeln ('You have ordered Reebok shoes.');
4: Writeln ('You have ordered Adidas shoes.');
Else
Writeln ('Wrong entry.');
End;
Write ('Press enter key to close.');
Readln;
End

Let us now look at the output.

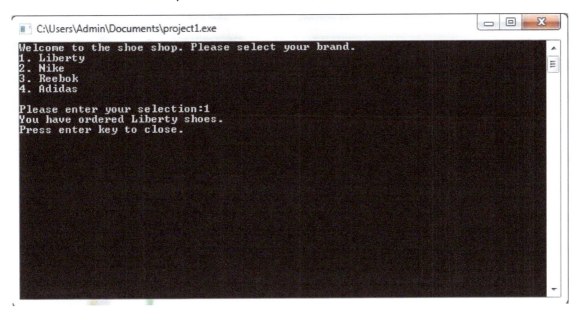

Depending upon the number we input, we get a suitable output. If we input 2, then we get a message that we have ordered Nike shoes. If we enter 3, then we get a message that we have ordered Reebok shoes. If we enter 4 then we get a message that we have ordered Adidas shoes. If we enter some other number then we get a message saying 'Wrong Entry'. This is when the control shifts to the 'else' part. The Case...of construct is closed with an end statement.

Loops (For, While, Repeat Until Loops)
Like conditional branching, practical situations demand the usage of iterative control structures as in loops. Using loops, we make a block of statements execute repeatedly until a condition evaluates to loop. Although the concept of an infinite loop is possible, it finds little use in actual programming.

There are three looping statements provided by PASCAL. They are:

1. For loop

2. While loop

3. repeat...until loop

First, we will go through the 'for' loop.

The FOR Loop

This loop is used to execute statements for a finite number of times and when we want to use counters. Consider this example:

Code:

```
Var
I: Integer;
Count: Integer;
Begin
Write ('Enter limit:');
Readln (Count);
For i:=1 to Count do
        Writeln ('Hello world!');
Write ('Press enter key to close');
Readln;
End.
```

The 'i' in the loop is known as a loop variable. Always use Integer, Byte, and Char for loop variables. Loop variables are also known as counters.

The output of this code segment is shown below:

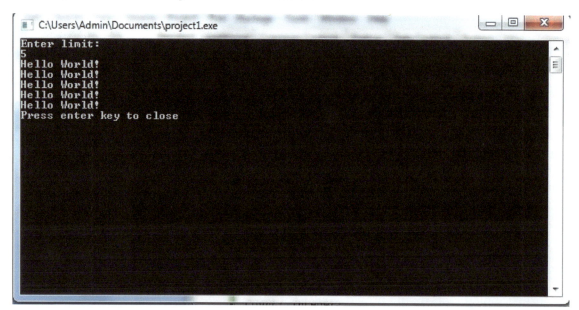

As we see, we input the limit as 5 and 'Hello World!' has been displayed 5 times.

We can also display the loop counter value in every iteration. For example, consider the following code segment.

Code:

```
Var
i: Integer;
Count: Integer;
Begin
Writeln('Enter limit:');
Readln(Count);
For i:=1 to Count do
Begin
Writeln('Hello World!');
Writeln('Iteration Number : ', i);
End;
Writeln('Press enter key to close.');
Readln;
End.
```

The output is shown below:

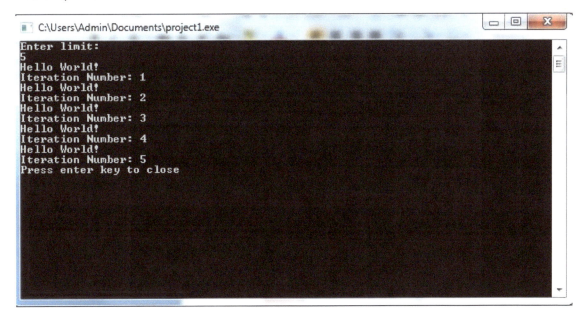

The 'begin' and 'end' statements inside the list are used to indicate that there are going to be multiple statements to be repeated using the loop.

Remember the multiplication program we did before. Using loops will make this easier. Let us see how.

Code:

```
Program MultTableWithForLoop;
{$mode objfpc}{$H+}
Uses
{$IFDEF UNIX}{IFDEF UseCThreads}
Cthreads,
{$ENDIF}{$ENDIF}
Classes
{ you can add units after this };
Var
X, i: Integer;
Begin
        Write ('Please input any number:');
ReadIn(X);
For i:=1 to 12 do
        Writeln (x, ' * ', i , ' = ', x * i);
Writeln('Press enter key to close.');
ReadIn;
End.
```

Here the writeln statement is executed 12 times.

The output is shown below:

Factorial of a number:

In mathematics, we have come across a term known as factorial of a number. It is actually the multiplication of a number by its predecessor down to the number 1.

For example: 5! = 5 * 4 * 3 * 2 * 1 = 120.

Let us see how we do this using loops.

Code:

```
Var
Fac, Num, i: Integer;
Begin
Writeln('Input a number:');
Readln(Num);
Fac:=1;
For i:=num downto 1 do
        Fac:=Fac * i;
Writeln('Factorial of ', Num, ' is ', Fac);
Writeln('Press enter key to close.');
Readln;
End.
```

Output:

The While Loop

In this loop, the condition is checked first. If it evaluates to true then the statements are executed. This loop is also called as top testing loop.

If the condition in the loop evaluates to false then the control skips the entire block to the statement next to the loop. If there are multiple statements which need to be executed repeatedly then we must enclose it within the 'begin…end' construct.

Let us now do the factorial program using while loop.

Code:

```
Var
Fac, Num, i: Integer;
Begin
Write('Please input any number:');
Readln(Num);
Fac:=1;
i:=Num;
while i>1 do
begin
        Fac:=Fac * i;
        i:i-1;
end;
writeln('Factorial of ', Num, ' is ', Fac);
Writeln('Press enter key to close.');
Readln;
End.
```

Output:

Repeat...Until loop:

Unlike the for loop, this loop does not make use of a counter. This loop executes the block atleast once. The condition is checked at the bottom of the loop. This is why it is known as the bottom testing loop. If the condition evaluates to true, the block is executed again otherwise the control skips to outside of the loop.

Let us do the shoe program using this loop.

Code:

```
Var
Meal: Char;
Price:=Integer;
Total:=Integer;
Begin
Total:=0;
Repeat
Writeln ('Welcome to the shoe shop. Please select your brand.');
Writeln ('1. Liberty (200 dollar)');
Writeln ('2. Nike (250 dollar)');
Writeln ('3. Reebok (235 dollar)');
Writeln ('4. Adidas (240 dollar)');
Writeln ;
Write ('Please enter your selection:');
Readln (Meal);
Case Meal of
'1': begin
writeln ('You have ordered Liberty shoes.');
```

```
price:=200;
end;
'2': begin
 writeln ('You have ordered Nike shoes.');
price:=250;
end;
'3': begin
writeln ('You have ordered Reebok shoes.');
price:=235;
end;
'4':begin
 Writeln ('You have ordered Adidas shoes.');
Price:=240;
End;
Else
begin
Writeln ('Wrong entry.');
Price:=0;
End;
End;
Total:=total + price;
Until(Meal='x') or (Meal='X');
Writeln('Total Price = ', total);
Write ('Press enter key to close.');
Readln;
End
```

Output:

Arrays:

Sometimes we want to store a bunch of values of the same type together. For this purpose we use arrays. An array is a container in which numerous variables are stored. Arrays can contain variables of the same data type only. Arrays store the variables in contiguous memory locations.

The first step is declaring an array. In Pascal, we do it in the following way:

Numbers: array [1...10] of Integer;

To access the elements of an array, we just refer to the index of the array. For example, if we want to put a value in the first variable in the array, then we write it as:

Numbers [1]:=30;

The indices of an array in Pascal start with 1 unlike most other programming languages.

In the next example, we will ask user to enter ten student marks and put them in an array. Then we will see who has passed or failed.

Code:

```
Var
Marks: array[1...10] of Integer;
i:Integer;
begin
for i:=1 to 10 do
begin
write('Input student number ', i , ' mark: ');
readln(Marks[i]);
end;
for i:=1 to 10 do
begin
write('Student number ', i, ' mark is : ', Marks[i]);
if Marks[i]>=40 then
writeln(' Pass');
else
writeln('Fail');
end;
writeln('Press enter key to close.')
readln;
end.
```

Executing this program will give the following output:

The user inputs ten values as is shown.

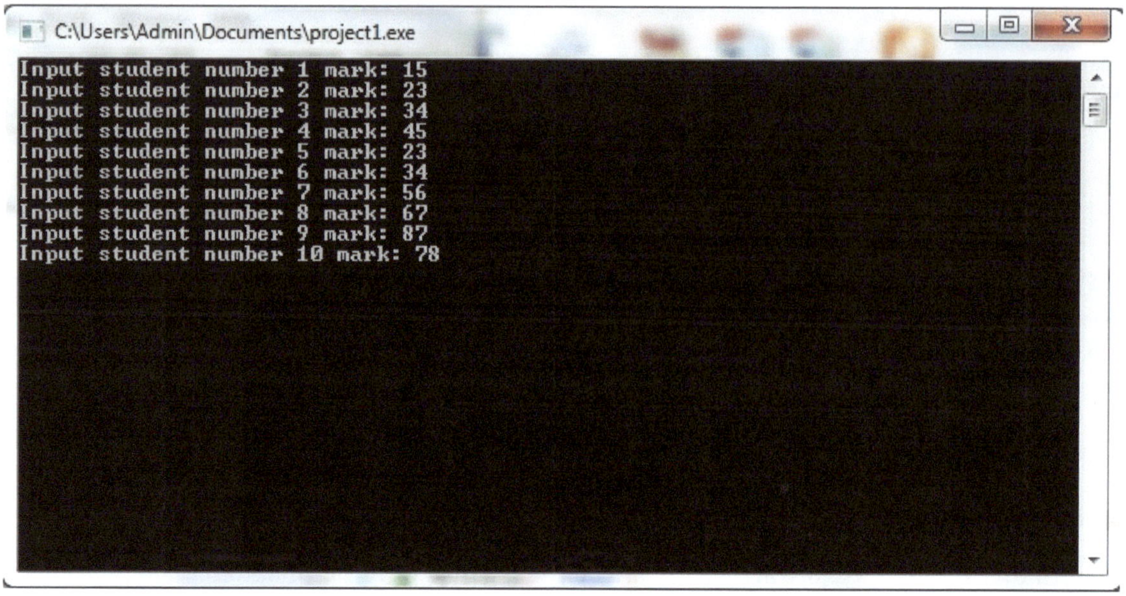

Press Enter after you include all the marks.

You get the following screen.

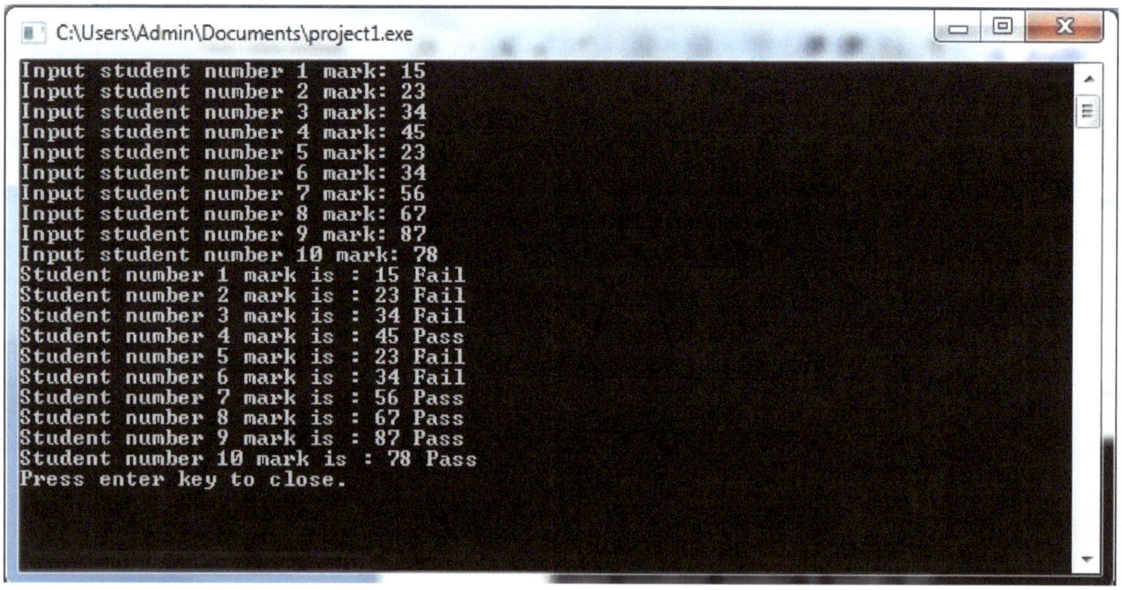

Subroutines

To assist in reusing common segments of programs subroutines have been developed. These routines are "sub-programs" that do a particular task that can be reused many times at different point within a main program or even by other programs. There are two basic types of subroutines, the procedure and the function. Each allows parameters to be passed into the subroutine so that the "sub-program" uses the values of those parameters to perform the task it is defined to do. This mechanism allows for the same "sub-program" to be used with different values in the parameters. There are multiple ways in which to pass the parameters to a subroutine, which is briefly discussed here. The function is differentiated from the procedure in that the function returns a value that is produced by that type of subroutine. Subroutines also cause the concept of "scope" to be introduced into programming. Scope has to do with the places where a particular variable is valid. This is an advanced topic that will be covered at a later time.

Procedures and Functions

A procedure is a subroutine that optionally takes input parameters and performs a task. It does not explicitly return a value to the program that called the procedure.

Function

A function is a subroutine that optionally takes input parameters and performs a task and returns a result. Though the input parameters are optional most function have input parameters in order to be useful. The value that is returned is defined to be a particular type.

Parameter Passing

Parameters are passed into subroutines by two basic methods. The parameters are either passed into the subroutine by value or by reference. Each of these types is used for different reasons, which will be covered at a later time.

By value – a parameter that is passed by value means that a copy of the value of the variable from the program that calls the subroutine is put in the parameter variable of the subroutine. The subroutine uses that copy of the variable's value within the subroutine but the value of the variable in the calling program is not affected.

By reference – a parameter that is passed by reference means that the location of the variable from the program that calls the subroutine is referred to by the parameter variable of the subroutine. The subroutine's parameter variable and the program's parameter variable are both located in the same place in memory. This implies that as the subroutine changes the value of the variable within the subroutine, the value of the variable in the calling program is also changed.

Return Values

A function returns a result of a particular type to the program that called the function. In the program that called the function a variable, either explicitly or implicitly will be assigned the returned value. The variable must be of the same type that the function returns.

Searching and Sorting:

We can write a program to search for a given element in an array. There are two types of search:

1. Linear Search

2. Binary Search

Linear Search:

In linear search, we traverse through the array and match the element we need found with each of the array indices. Once found, we display the element. The following code snippet will tell us how to do linear search.

Code:

```
Var
i, Num: Integer;
numbers: array [1..10] of Integer;
begin
writeln('Enter the elements of array:');
for i:=1 to 10 do
begin
writeln('Enter element no: ',i);
readln(numbers[i]);
end;
writeln('Enter number you want searched:');
Readln(Num);
For i:=1 to 10 do
Begin
If numbers[i]=num then
Writeln('Number found at index no ', i)
End;
Writeln('Press enter to close.');
Readln;
End.
```

When this program is executed we get the following input screen.

According to the array values, the number 5 should be present at index 5. Let us see whether we get the same output.

Binary Search:

Binary search involves repeatedly cutting the part of the list that one is looking for in half, until one either finds the element one is looking for, or the part of the list that one is looking has become empty. Binary search starts by comparing the element one is looking for with the element mid way down the list. If the list is empty, one can return failure immediately; if this element is identical to the one we are looking for, then we immediately. Otherwise, and assuming that the list is sorted in ascending order, if the element one is looking for is smaller than the element in the middle, one repeats the process for the first half of the list; if the element is larger, then one repeats the process for the second half of the list. Clearly, if the list is sorted in descending order, then this has to be reversed.

Code:

```
var

A:Array [1..80] of integer;

b,c,e,i,n,m:integer;

d:real;

begin

clrscr;

writeln("ENTER THE LENGTH OF ARRAY ");

read(n);

writeln("ENTER ",n," NUMBERS ");

for i:=1 to n do

read(A[i]);

b:=A[1];

e:=A[n];

d:=(b+e)/2;

m:=trunc(d);

writeln("ENTER THE NUMBER TO BE SEARCHED ");

read(c);

while (A[m]<>c) and (b=e) do

begin

if c>0 then
```

e:=m-1

else

b:=m+1;

m:=trunc(d);

end;

if c=A[m] then

writeln("ELEMENT IS FOUND ")

else

writeln("ELEMENT NOT FOUND ");

end.

Output:

Enter the length of the array:
5
Enter 5 numbers:
1
3
4
6
7

Enter the number to be searched:
6

ELEMENT FOUND

SORTING:

Sorting is a process where the values in an array are arranged in ascending or descending order.

There are numerous sorting methods available to us. Some of them are listed below:
1. Selection Sort
2. Bubble Sort
3. Insertion Sort
4. Radix Sort

5. Merge Sort
6. Heap Sort
7. Quick Sort
8. Bucket sort

In this lesson we will only be dealing with selection and bubble sort.

SELECTION SORT:

The intuition behind selection sort is relatively straightforward. Simply find the smallest element in the list and swap it with the element at the front of the list. Then repeat the procedure starting at position 1 in the list, find the smallest element in the remainder of the list and swap it with the element in position 1. We then repeat the procedure starting at position 2 and so on until we have sorted the entire list.

Code:

```
program project1;

{$APPTYPE CONSOLE}

{.$DEFINE DYNARRAY} // remove '.' to compile with dynamic array

type
  TItem = Integer;   // declare ordinal type for array item
{$IFDEF DYNARRAY}
  TArray = array of TItem;        // dynamic array
{$ELSE}
  TArray = array[0..15] of TItem;  // static array
{$ENDIF}

procedure SelectionSort(var A: TArray);
var
  Item: TItem;
  I, J, M: Integer;

begin
  for I:= Low(A) to High(A) - 1 do begin
    M:= I;
    for J:= I + 1 to High(A) do
      if A[J] < A[M] then M:= J;
    Item:= A[M];
    A[M]:= A[I];
    A[I]:= Item;
  end;
end;
```

```
var
  A: TArray;
  I: Integer;

begin
{$IFDEF DYNARRAY}
  SetLength(A, 16);
{$ENDIF}
  for I:= Low(A) to High(A) do
    A[I]:= Random(100);
  for I:= Low(A) to High(A) do
    Write(A[I]:3);
  Writeln;
  SelectionSort(A);
  for I:= Low(A) to High(A) do
    Write(A[I]:3);
  Writeln;
  Readln;
end.
```

Here in this program we have used dynamic values inside an array and the concept of procedures. Procedures are similar to functions. They isolate a block of code so that they can be used by the main code whenever desired. Breaking a program into functions is one of the best practices of structured programming.

The output of this code segment is:

C:\Users\Admin\Documents\project1.exe

```
 54 59 71 84 60 85 54 84 42 62 64 38 43 29 89  5
  5 29 38 42 43 54 54 59 60 62 64 71 84 84 85 89
```

BUBBLE SORT:

Bubble Sort is probably the easiest sorting algorithm.

The basic idea behind the bubble sort algorithm is as follows: Compare the last two elements in the list and swap them if the second element is smaller than the first. Then consider the two elements before them and repeat the procedure. Process all adjacent pairs of elements in the list until you reach the front of the list. A little thought should show that, at this point, the smallest element has "bubbled" up to the front of the list. We now repeat the process, again starting at the end of the list. However, since the smallest element is already at the front, we can stop when we reach the second element in the list. Again, it should be clear that, at this stage, the second element in the list is the second smallest element in the list. We keep repeating these passes through the list until the entire list has been sorted.

Code:

```
program project1;

{$mode objfpc}{$H+}

uses
  {$IFDEF UNIX}{$IFDEF UseCThreads}
  cthreads,
  {$ENDIF}{$ENDIF}
  Classes
  { you can add units after this };
Var i, j, temp : Integer;

Numbers: array[1 .. 10] of Integer;
Size: Integer;


Begin
Size:=10;
For i:=1 to 10 do
Readln(numbers[i]);

 For i := size-1 DownTo 1 do
  For j := 2 to i do
   If (numbers[j-1] > numbers[j]) then
    Begin
     temp := numbers[j-1];
     numbers[j-1] := numbers[j];
     numbers[j] := temp;
    End;
For i:=1 to 10 do
writeln(numbers[i]);
End.
```

Output:

2
4
7
6
5
3
1
8
9
10
1
2
3
4
5
6
7
8
9
10

Quick Sort:

Quick sort is a recursive algorithm. The idea behind the algorithm is

- Choose an arbitrary element of the list as the pivot;
- Divide the list into two sub-lists;
- The list of all elements smaller than the pivot;
- The list of all elements larger than the pivot.

Sort the two sub-lists;

Form a new list consisting of the first sorted sub-list followed by the pivot followed by the second sorted sub-list.

Clearly, since this is a recursive algorithm, we have to be careful about when to terminate the recursion. There are three conditions under which the recursion can terminate:

When the list is empty

When the list contains 1 element

When the list contains 2 elements, in which case we swap them if necessary.

Code:

```
Procedure QSort(numbers : Array of Integer;
        left : Integer; right : Integer);
Var pivot, l_ptr, r_ptr : Integer;


Begin
```

```
l_ptr := left;
r_ptr := right;
pivot := numbers[left];
While (left < right) do
 Begin
  While ((numbers[right] >= pivot) AND (left < right)) do
   right := right - 1;
  If (left <> right) then
   Begin
    numbers[left] := numbers[right];
    left := left + 1;
   End;
  While ((numbers[left] <= pivot) AND (left < right)) do
   left := left + 1;
  If (left <> right) then
   Begin
    numbers[right] := numbers[left];
    right := right - 1;
   End;
 End;
numbers[left] := pivot;
pivot := left;
left := l_ptr;
right := r_ptr;
If (left < pivot) then
 QSort(numbers, left, pivot-1);
If (right > pivot) then
 QSort(numbers, pivot+1, right);
End;
Procedure QuickSort(numbers : Array of Integer; size : Integer);
Begin
 QSort(numbers, 0, size-1);
End;
```

FILES:

Files form a very important part of operating systems. Many operating system components , information and data are represented in files.

Operations on files are managed by the operating system.

Files are classified depending on the perspective. For now, we will group files under these two categories:

1. Data Files.
2. Executable Files.

However, depending upon their contents, files can be classified into these categories:

1. Text Files: They contain simple text which can be written into or read from by using any simple tool including operating system command lines.

2. Binary Files: These are more complex files and need special applications to open them.

There is this another way of classifying files. This is based on the access type.

1. Sequential Files: The best example one can give of a sequential file is a text file. It has no fixed size record. Each line has its own length. For this reason, we open the file only in read-only mode or writing-only. Here, we can only append to the end of file.

2. Random Access Files: This type of file ha a fixed size record. A record is the smallest unit of a file. It can be an integer, byte, or string. It can also be user defined. In case of random access files, we can perform both the read and write operations simultaneously.

Text Files:

We must write them only in a forward direction. There are three modes we must know about when opening this sort of a file: Read, Write, and Append.

Here we will display the contents of file selected by user.

Code:

```
Program ReadFile;
{$mode objfpc}{$H+}
Uses
{$IFDEF UNIX}{$IFDEF UseCThreads}
Cthreads,
{$ENDIF}{$ENDIF}
Classes, sysUtils
{ you  can use units after this };
Var
FileName: String;
F: TextFile;
Line: String;
Begin
        Write('Input a text file name:');
        Readln(FileName);
        If FileExists(FileName) then
        Begin
                AssignFile(F, FileName); //Link file variable with physical file
                Reset (F); //put file mode to read
                While not Eof(F) do
                Begin
                        Readln(F,Line); //read a line from file
                        Writeln(Line);
                End;
        CloseFile(F); //Release file connection
End
Else
        Writeln('File does not exist');
Write('Press Enter key to close.');
Readln;
End.
```

In the above program, we see new things. Let us understand their meaning.

1. F: TextFile

TextFile is a type which is used to declare a text file variable. This variable is usually linked to a physical text file.

2. if FileExists(FileName) then

FileExists is a function which is present in the SysUtils unit. It checks whether the file given as a parameter to it exists or not. It returns true if found.

3. AssignFile(F, FileName)

Once we have found out that the file exists in the hard drive, we use this procedure to link the text file variable we created to the physical file.

4. Reset (F);

This procedure opens text files for reading purposes only. It puts the reading pointer to the first character of the file.

5. while not Eof(f) do

The Eof function will return true if the end of file is reached.

Now, we will learn how to create a new file and write into it.

Code:

```
Var
FileName:String;
F:TextFile;
Line:String;
ReadyToCreate:Boolean;
Ans:Char;
i: Integer;
begin
write('Input a file name:');
readln(FileName);
if FileExists(FileName) then
begin
write('File Already Exist, do you want to overwrite(Y/N)?');
Readln(Ans);
If upcase(Ans)='Y' then
ReadyToCreate:=True;
Else
ReadyToCreate:=False;
End
Else
ReadyToCreate:=True;
```

```
If ReadyToCreate then
Begin
AssignFile(F, FileName);
Rewrite(F);
Writeln('Please input file contents line by line. When you finish, write % and press enter.');
i:=1;
repeat
write('Line # ',  i, ':');
Inc(i);
Readln(Line);
If Line <> '%' then
Writeln(F, Line);
Until Line= '%';
CloseFile(F);
End
Else
Writeln('Doing nothing…');
Write('Press enter key to close.');
Readln;
End.
```

In this example, we came across these new things:

1. Boolean Type:

Boolean is a data type. Variables of this type can have only either of the two values: True or False. These variables can be used directly anywhere a condition is used.

2. UpCase Function:

This function converts a lower case character into an upper case character.

3. Rewrite Procedure;

The Rewrite procedure is used to create a new empty file.

4. Writeln(F,…) Procedure:

This procedure inputs text into a file.

5. Inc Procedure:

This procedure is used to increment the value of an integer by one.

Appending Text Files:

Code:

```
Var
FileName: String;
F: TextFile;
Line: String;
i: Integer;
begin
```

```
Write('Input an existing file name.');
Readln(FileName);
If FileExists(FileName) then
Begin
        AssignFile(F, FileName);
        Append(F);
        Writeln('Please input file contents line by line. When you finish, write % and press enter.');
        i:=1;
        repeat
                write('Line # ',  i, ':');
                Inc(i);
                Readln(Line);
                If Line <> '%' then
                        Writeln(F, Line);
        Until Line='%';
        CloseFile(F);
End
Else
        Writeln('File does not exist');
Write('Press enter key to close..');
Readln;
End.
```

Random Access Files:

There are two types of random access files. They are:

1. **Typed Files**.

2. **Untyped Files**.

Typed Files:

These files contain records of the same size and which have data of the same type.

We will now create a file of new student marks records.

Code:

```
Var
F: file of Byte;
Mark: Byte;
Begin
        AssignFile(F, 'marks.dat');
        Rewrite(F);
        Writeln('Please input student marks, write 0 to exit.');
        Repeat
                Write('Input mark:');
                Readln(Mark);
                If Mark<>0 then
                        Write(F, Mark);
```

```
                Until Mark=0;
                CloseFile(F);
                Write('Press enter key to close.');
                Readln;
        End.
```

Here we have use F: file of Byte. This indicates that the file contains data of the type Byte. The data can hold values from 0 to 255.

To write records into the file, we use the Write function instead of Writeln.

Now, we will write a program to read contents from this file.

Code:

```
Program ReadFile;
{$mode objfpc}{$H+}
Uses
{$IFDEF UNIX}{IFDEF UseCThreads}
Cthreads,
{$ENDIF}{$ENDIF}
Classes, sysUtils
{ you can use units after this };
Var
F: file of Byte;
Mark: Byte;
Begin
        AssignFile(F, 'marks.dat');
        If FileExists('marks.dat') then
        Begin
                Reset(F);
                While not Eof(F) do
                Begin
                        Read(F, Mark);
                        Writeln('Mark: ', Mark);
                End
                CloseFile(F);
        End
        Else
                Writeln('File not found');

        Write('Press enter key to close.');
        Readln;
End.
```

Now we will append contents to this file.

Code:

```
Program ReadFile;
{$mode objfpc}{$H+}
```

```pascal
Uses
{$IFDEF UNIX}{IFDEF UseCThreads}
Cthreads,
{$ENDIF}{$ENDIF}
Classes, sysUtils
{ you  can use units after this };
Var
F: file of Byte;
Mark: Byte;
Begin
        AssignFile(F, 'marks.dat');
        If FileExists('marks.dat') then
        Begin
                FileMode:=2;
                Reset(F);
                Seek(F, FileSize(F));
                Writeln('Please input marks, write 0 to exit.');
                Repeat
                        Write('Input mark:');
                        Readln(Mark);
                        If Mark<>0 then
                                Write(F, Mark);
                Until Mark=0;
                CloseFile(F);
        End
        Else
                Writeln('File not found.');

        Write('Press enter key to close...');
        Readln;
End.
```

Here file mode 2 indicates that the file is ready for the read/write mode. The Seek procedure moves the read/write pointer to the end of file. The FileSize function returns the number of records currently in the file. It is used in the Seek procedure.

Now we will learn how to copy contents from one file to another.

Code:

```pascal
Program ReadFile;
{$mode objfpc}{$H+}
Uses
{$IFDEF UNIX}{IFDEF UseCThreads}
Cthreads,
{$ENDIF}{$ENDIF}
Classes, sysUtils
{ you  can use units after this };
Var
SourceName, DestName: String;
```

```
SourceF, DestF: file of Byte;
Block: Byte;
Begin
Writeln('File Copy Example.');
Write('Input source file name:');
Readln(SourceName);

Write('Input destination file name:');
Readln(DestName);

If FileExists(SourceName) then
Begin
        AssignFile(SourceF, SourceName);
        AssignFile(DestF, DestName);

        FileMode:=0;
        Reset(SourceF);
        Rewrite(DestF);

        Writeln('Copying..');

        While not Eof(SourceF) do
        Begin
                Read(SourceF, Block);
                Write(DestF, Block);
        End;
        CloseFile(SourceF);
        CloseFile(DestF);
End
Else

        Writeln('Source file does not exist.');

        Write('Copying completed..press enter key to close.');
        Readln;
End.
```

Untyped Files:

Untyped Files are random access files that have a fixed record length. However, they are not linked to any data type. Instead, they treat data (records) as an array.

Copying files using untyped files is a lot more faster than using typed files. We will see the program how to do that.

Code:

```
Program ReadFile;
{$mode objfpc}{$H+}
Uses
{$IFDEF UNIX}{IFDEF UseCThreads}
Cthreads,
```

```pascal
{$ENDIF}{$ENDIF}
Classes, sysUtils
{ you  can use units after this };

Var
SourceName, DestName : String;
SourceF, DestF: File;
Block: array[0 .. 1023] of Byte;
NumRead: Integer;

Begin
        Writeln('File Copy Example.');
        Write('Input source file name:');
        Readln(SourceName);

        Write('Input destination file name:');
        Readln(DestName);

        If FileExists(SourceName) then
        Begin
                AssignFile(SourceF, SourceName);
                AssignFile(DestF, DestName);

                FileMode:=0;
                Reset(SourceF, 1);
                Rewrite(SourceF, 1);

                Writeln('Copying...');
                While not Eof(SourceF) do
                Begin
                        BlockRead(SourceF, Block, SizeOf(Block), NumRead);
                        BlockWrite(DestF, Block, NumRead);
                End;

                CloseFile(SourceF);
                CloseFile(DestF);
        End
        Else
                Writeln('Source File does not exist.');

        Writeln('Copying finished...Press Enter key to close...');
        Readln;
End.
```

TRACE TABLES

A **trace table** is a table with one column for each variable used and one column for the output. A cell shows a change in a variable or the output as the program is executed. There are three ways to fill out a trace table.

1.

Use one row for each change.

Advantage: shows the order of events.

Disadvantage: takes up a lot of space.

A	output
2	
4	
	4
6	
	6

```
A = 2
while A < 5
    A = A + 2
    msgbox str(A)
wend
```

2.

Use one row for each time the loop runs.

Advantage: takes up less space.

Disadvantage: cannot be used if a variable changes more than once in the loop.

A	output
2	
4	4
6	6

3.

Use next cell when there is a change.

Advantage: takes up little space.

Disadvantage: Does not show the order of events.

A	output
2	4
4	6
6	4

dry-run	A manual traversal/run of a program using a trace table.
stepping through a program	A good debugging tool is to run a program one instruction at a time. Press F8 to get started and then click Locals Window on the View menu to see how the variables change every time you press F8 to execute the next instruction.
source code	Program written in a computer language.

object code	Machine language program produced by a compiler.
compiler	A computer program, which translates a high-level language program (the source) into machine code (the object code, an executable file).
interpreter	A computer program which analyses and executes a source program one statement at a time; without converting it to object code.
loader	A computer program, which copies an object program held on backing store into main store.
executing	A program is executed or run when the computer carries out the program's instructions.

Watches:

One can trace the execution of a program in Lazarus. There are Step Into and Step Over functions available to us if we ever want to know the details of programming. Often it is helpful to a programmer as it helps in debugging procedure.

The Step Into function is a menu item in the Run Menu. To access, click Run -> Step Into. Alternatively press F7. Step Into executes every line of the program.

The Step Over function is a menu item in the Run Menu. To access, click Run -> Step Over. Alternatively, press F8.

Program Documentation:

The program documentation is like a comprehensive procedural description of a program. It shows how a program is written. The program documentation describes exactly what a program intends to achieve. There are two kinds of program documentation:

1. Internal Documentation

2. External Documentation

Internal Documentation

Internal Documentation involves meaningful variable names, comments, indentation etc…

Variable Names:

All variable names must follow the rules outlined below:

1. They must begin with a letter or an underscore.

2. They can contain only letters, numbers, or underscores.

3. They cannot have blank spaces.

Examples of illegal variable names: 5BREADTH, AB 3, Vee.Hive, etc..

Comments:

Comments are piece of code which are completely discarded by the compiler. They exist only to help the programmer and to provide him with an easy reference.

In the early days, (* and *) were used to indicate comments. However, they have been replaced by { and }. These are mostly used for multi-line comments.

// is used for a single line comment.

Examples:

// This is a Hello World function

{

       This is a hello world function.

       You see hello world as output.

}

Indentation:

You should always indent two spaces for all indentation levels. In other words, the first level of indentation is two spaces, the second level four spaces, the third level 6 spaces, etc. Never use tab characters.

There are few exceptions. The reserved words unit, users, type, interface, implementation, initialization and finalization should always be flush with the margin. The final end statement at the end of a unit should be flush with the margin.

External Documentation:

External documentation is to help the user of the system to understand how the software works. It is a book like document having the following contents:

1. Cover page.
2. Title page and copyright page.
3. A preface covering the details of relevant documents and information on how to navigate through the guide.
4. Contents page in tabular form.
5. A guide section on how to use the main functions.
6. Troubleshooting section detailing the errors which might occur and how to solve them.
7. A FAQ document.
8. Where to find further help and contact details.
9. A glossary.

PASCAL ERROR CODES

The following error codes are predefined:

Code	Meaning
1	Invalid function number
2	File not found
3	Path not found
4	Too many open files
5	File access denied
6	Invalid file handle
12	Invalid file access code
15	Invalid drive number
16	Cannot remove current directory
17	Cannot rename across drives
18	No more files
100	Disk read error
101	Disk write error
102	File not assigned
103	File not open
104	File not open for input
105	File not open for output
106	Invalid numeric format
150	Disk is write protected
151	Bad drive request structure length
152	Drive not ready

154	CRC error in data
156	Disk seek error
157	Unknown media type
158	Sector not found
159	Printer out of paper
160	Device write fault
161	Device read fault
162	Hardware failure
200	Division by zero
201	Range check error
202	Stack overflow error
203	Heap overflow error
204	Invalid pointer operation
205	Floating point overflow
206	Floating point underflow
207	Invalid floating point operation
208	Overlay manager not installed
209	Overlay file read error
210	Object not initialized
211	Call to abstract method
212	Stream registration error
213	Collection index out of range

214	Collection overflow error
215	Arithmetic overflow error
216	General protection fault
217	Invalid operation code
227	Assertion failed
300	File IO error
301	Non matched array bounds
302	Non local procedure pointer
303	Procedure pointer out of scope
304	Function not implemented
305	Breakpoint error
306	Break by Ctrl/C
307	Break by Ctrl/Break
308	Break by other process
309	No floating point coprocessor
310	Invalid Variant type operation

CASE STUDY: MASQUERADERS

Using the programming language Pascal, write program code to implement the algorithm you wrote in Unit 2.

Solution:
The program is given below:

Program Program1;
{$mode objfpc}{$H+}

```
Uses
{$IFDEF UNIX}{$IFDEF UseCThreads}
Cthreads,
{$ENDIF}{$ENDIF}
Classes, sysUtils
{ you  can use units after this };

Var
Section1_cnt, section2_cnt, section3_cnt, section4_cnt, section5_cnt: Integer;
Section1_sum, section2_sum, section3_sum, section4_sum, section5_sum: Integer;
I, j: Integer;
Member:array[1..50,1..2] of String;
Name: String;
Amount: Integer;
k: Integer;


begin
        section1_cnt:=0;
        section2_cnt:=0;
        section3_cnt:=0;
        section4_cnt:=0;
        section5_cnt:=0;
        section1_sum:=0;
        section2_sum:=0;
        section3_sum:=0;
        section4_sum:=0;
        section5_sum:=0;
        i:=1;
        j:=1;

    For i:=1 to 2 do
    begin
       for j:=1 to 2 do
       begin

          if(j=1) then
          begin
          Writeln('Input Member Name:');
          Readln(Name);
          Member [i, j]:=Name;
           end;
          if (j = 2) then
          begin
             Writeln('Enter amount:');
             Read(Amount);
             if (Amount = 160) then
             begin
                Section1_cnt:=Section1_cnt + 1;
                Member[i, j]:='1';
                Writeln('Member belongs to section 1');
```

```pascal
            Section1_sum:=Section1_sum + Amount

        end
        else if (Amount=220) then
        begin
            Section2_cnt:=Section2_cnt + 1;
            Member[i, j]:='2';
            Writeln('Member belongs to section 2');
            Section2_sum:=Section2_sum + Amount
        end
        else if (Amount=280) then
        begin
            section3_cnt:=section3_cnt + 1;
            Member[i, j]:='3';
            Writeln('Member belongs to section 3');
            section3_sum:=section3_sum+Amount
        end
        else if (Amount=350) then
        begin
            section4_cnt:=section4_cnt + 1;
            Member[i, j]:='4';
            Writeln('Member belongs to section 4');
            section4_sum:=section4_sum + Amount
        end
        else if (Amount = 425) then
        begin
            section5_cnt:=section5_cnt+1;
            Member[i, j]:='5';
            Writeln('Member belongs to section 5');
            section5_sum:=section5_sum+Amount
        end
        else
        begin
            Writeln('Member not paid amount');
        end;

    end;
  end;
end;

    Writeln ('---------------------------------------------SECTION OUTPUT------------------------------');
    Writeln ('Section Number                 Section Count');
    Writeln ('                1              ', section1_cnt);
    Writeln ('                2              ',section2_cnt);
    Writeln ('                3              ',section3_cnt);
    Writeln ('                4              ', section4_cnt);
    Writeln ('                5              ',section5_cnt);

    For k:=1 to 10 do
begin
        Writeln ('Member Name:', Member[k, j], 'Section Name', Member[k, j+1]);
```

```pascal
            j:=1;
      end;

   Writeln('Section Number                    Section Amount');
      Writeln('              1                    ',section1_sum);
      Writeln('              2                    ',section2_sum);
      Writeln('              3                    ',section3_sum);
      Writeln('              4                    ',section4_sum);
      Writeln('              5                    ',section5_sum);

End.
```

Chapter Summary:

In this chapter, we learned about:

1. The different generations of programming languages.

2. How to use PASCAL programs.

3. How to create arrays and use them.

4. How to create files and handle them.

5. The different error codes.

INDEX

1s 79

Arrays 116

BUBBLE SORT 3, 126

C 2, 16, 19, 79, 80

Chapter Objectives 1, 2, 3, 16, 48, 77, 80, 84, 86, 88, 91, 92, 119, 145

Characteristics of Machine Language 79

Cobol 6, 8, 57, 80, 113

Code Listing 3, 101

commands 53, 54, 57, 58, 79, 83, 141

Comments 141

compiler 141

Data Types 3, 91

Dry Run 83

dry-run 58, 140

easily maintained 78

English like statements 80

Executable Files 3, 130

Factorial of a number 112

faster 79

FILES 3, 126, 129

Fourth generation language (4GL) 80

Function 3, 121

High-level language(s) 79

Internal Documentation 141

Linear Search 122

loader 141

logical error 83, 140, 141

Loops (For, While, Repeat Until Loops) 3, 103

Machine language 77, 79, 84, 100, 130

MASQUERADERS 2, 3, 4, 71, 145

Meaning10, 19, 20, 36, 40, 88, 89, 90, 91, 93, 94, 96, 97, 98, 100, 101, 102, 103, 104, 108, 109, 110, 112,113, 115, 116, 117, 119, 122, 124, 126, 128, 129, 131, 132, 133, 134, 135, 136, 137, 143

Pascal 80

Pascal Editor and Library 2, 83

PASCAL ERROR CODES 142

Pascal Programs 86

programming language 2, 79

Programming Languages 77, 148

reliable 78, 98

Return Values 3, 121

robust 78

runtime error 83

Second generation language 79

short codes 2, 11, 79, 80

Solution 148

SORTING..7, 11, 122, 123
source code 140
STO 79
String...3, 97
such as C, Cobol or Fortran..80
Summary...72
testing...82
TRACE TABLES..134, 137
Translators..80
Typed Files..131, 134
Watches...83, 84, 92, 141